Also from Westphalia Press
westphaliapress.org

The Idea of the Digital University

Dialogue in the Roman-Greco World

The History of Photography

International or Local Ownership?: Security Sector Development in Post-Independent Kosovo

Lankes, His Woodcut Bookplates

Opportunity and Horatio Alger

The Role of Theory in Policy Analysis

The Little Confectioner

Non-Profit Organizations and Disaster

The Idea of Neoliberalism: The Emperor Has Threadbare Contemporary Clothes

Social Satire and the Modern Novel

Ukraine vs. Russia: Revolution, Democracy and War: Selected Articles and Blogs, 2010-2016

James Martineau and Rebuilding Theology

A Strategy for Implementing the Reconciliation Process

Issues in Maritime Cyber Security

A Different Dimension: Reflections on the History of Transpersonal Thought

Iran: Who Is Really In Charge?

Contracting, Logistics, Reverse Logistics: The Project, Program and Portfolio Approach

Unworkable Conservatism: Small Government, Freemarkets, and Impracticality

Springfield: The Novel

Lariats and Lassos

Ongoing Issues in Georgian Policy and Public Administration

Growing Inequality: Bridging Complex Systems, Population Health and Health Disparities

Designing, Adapting, Strategizing in Online Education

Pacific Hurtgen: The American Army in Northern Luzon, 1945

Natural Gas as an Instrument of Russian State Power

New Frontiers in Criminology

Feeding the Global South

Beijing Express: How to Understand New China

The Rise of the Book Plate: An Exemplative of the Art

The Jesters

A Simple Story in Four Acts of Verse from the French of Miguel Zamacoïs

---

by John N. Raphael

WESTPHALIA PRESS
An Imprint of Policy Studies Organization

The Jesters: A Simple Story in Four Acts of Verse from the French
of Miguel Zamacoïs
All Rights Reserved © 2018 by Policy Studies Organization

Westphalia Press
An imprint of Policy Studies Organization
1527 New Hampshire Ave., NW
Washington, D.C. 20036
info@ipsonet.org

ISBN-13: 978-1-63391-649-4
ISBN-10: 1-63391-649-9

Cover design by Jeffrey Barnes:
jbarnesbook.design

Daniel Gutierrez-Sandoval, Executive Director
PSO and Westphalia Press

Updated material and comments on this edition
can be found at the Westphalia Press website:
www.westphaliapress.org

THE JESTERS

THE JESTERS

A SIMPLE STORY IN FOUR ACTS OF VERSE

ADAPTED FROM THE FRENCH OF

MIGUEL ZAMACOÏS

BY

JOHN N. RAPHAEL

NEW YORK
BRENTANO'S
1908

COPYRIGHT, 1908, BY BRENTANO'S

D. B. UPDIKE, THE MERRYMOUNT PRESS, BOSTON

THE FIRST ACT

DRAMATIS PERSONAE

RENÉ DE CHANCENAC (*afterwards* CHICOT)
NICOLE
SOLANGE DE MAUTPRÉ
VULCANO
BARON DE MAUTPRÉ
ROBERT DE BELFONTE (*afterwards* NARCISSUS)
OLIVER
BAROCO ⎫
JACK PUDDING ⎬ *jesters*
HILARIUS ⎭
JACQUES ⎫
JULIAN ⎬ *servants of the* BARON DE MAUTPRÉ
PIERRE ⎭
HUBERT, *servant to* RENÉ DE CHANCENAC
A Pedlar, &c.

The story runs its course in France in the year 1557

THE JESTERS
ACT FIRST

The scene is a large hall in a picturesque old castle which has seen better days. A large window at the back of the stage opens on to a broad stone terrace, overgrown with moss and showing signs of age and dilapidation. Green creepers and roses frame the window, through which a bright sun shines and pitilessly discloses the lack of comfort and need of repairs. The furniture, of which there is very little, bears eloquent witness to the poverty of the BARON DE MAUTPRÉ, *owner of the castle. There is a staircase on the right, leading up to a small door. Under the stairs is another small door opening on to the stairs down to the cellar. Both of these staircases are used.*

At the rise of the curtain JACQUES, JULIAN, PIERRE *and* NICOLE *are discovered.*

JULIAN

Eighteen months' wages due, and not a penny piece.
(*To* JACQUES) Speak up for us.

JACQUES
'T is time this worrying should cease;

Because, forsooth, I can say what I want to say,
I have to risk my place by dunning for our pay.

NICOLE

You are of all of us the cleverest, you see.
You are the one to speak. You speak convincingly.

JACQUES

No! I am tired of it. My voice alone is heard,
I am the grumbler. You never vouchsafe a word.
You're bright enough, Nicole. Julian is not a dunce.
When the time comes to-day, let's all four speak at once.

PIERRE

Hush! Dr. Oliver!

Enter OLIVER

OLIVER

    Come, come, my friends, to work!
For the last day or two everyone seems to shirk
All that there is to do.

  (*To* JULIAN) What have *you* done to-day?

JULIAN

Fed the ass.

OLIVER, *to* NICOLE
Have you swept?

ACT FIRST

NICOLE, *crossly*

Ev'ryone's in the way.

OLIVER, *laughing*

Dame Nicole's out of sorts.

(*To all*) Come, come, there's work to do.
Put off these sulky airs, set to it all of you.
(*Pointing to stones which are heaped up under the archway at the back of the stage*)
Where do these stones come from?

JACQUES

(*Pointing to the arch*) They fell out in the night.

OLIVER

Ah, yes! The castle's old.
(*Looking up*) Well, we'll have this put right.
But you must not forget, when you pass; more may fall.

JACQUES

All the walls shed their stones. This is no house at all.

OLIVER

What is it, pray?

JACQUES

A sieve. When the wind blows at night,

None of us close an eye; some are half dead with fright.

OLIVER

Why?

JACQUES

Why? Because, instead of crumbling bits away,
The whole house will fall in when it blows hard one day.

NICOLE

Yes. And that's not the worst, for if the walls could tell
What they have heard us say — all our complaints —
(*She sighs*) Ah! well!

OLIVER

You are cared for and fed! What more can you desire?

JACQUES

Wages!

NICOLE

Yes!

PIERRE *and* JULIAN

Yes!

JACQUES

We have all earned and want our hire.

ACT FIRST

OLIVER

Ah! All your heads are thick and all your hearts are hard
As the stones fallen there.
(*Struck by a sudden idea, to* JACQUES)
With them we'll pave the yard.
(*To the malcontents*)
Surely you know how poor all of the tenants be,
And that the harvest's poor, doubling their poverty!
None of the rents are paid our coffers here to fill.
Why, for those of three years ago we're waiting still!
What does the Baron do? Summon his men-at-arms,
Harry the countryside, go down and sack the farms?
No. Many times have I seen him in anger rise,
Ready for war, then pause, and with tears in his eyes
Shake his head, smile, and then: "Oliver," he will say,
"Call me my soldiers back."

JACQUES

Soldiers, but where are they?
Every day we hear trumpeters sound the call,
But when the call does sound there are no men at all.
No doubt the farmer hears, trembles there on his farm,

Thinks you have men, but we know and feel no
   alarm.
Ah! Mautpré's tiger-claw no longer strikes to kill,
And when the pow'r is lost, what is the use of will?
Army forsooth! Our lord owns just one man, and
   he
Is all our foot, our horse, infantry, cavalry,
General, Colonel, drums, linesman, and sentry-go.
And what a man for all these posts is Vulcano!
This great Italian who bullies and bates us all,
Half soldier, half bravo! When he patrols the wall,
Down in the country lanes villagers pause and say:
"Strange that we only see one sentry ev'ry day."

OLIVER

Do they say that?

NICOLE

            They do, and many want to know
Why the same man is always upon sentry-go.

OLIVER

Ah, yes! The mice may squeak, but when the cat
   appears,
Into their holes they pop—Vulcano each one fears.

NICOLE

Vulcano? What, that great long scraggy braggart!
   Why,

ACT FIRST

Not a field mouse, *I'm* sure, before his sword would
 fly.
Don't you remember how, gone to collect the
 dues,
Vulcano hurried back pelted with wooden shoes?

OLIVER

Take care he hears you not!

JACQUES

                      None of us for him care,
But can *you* say as much? Else why do you for-
 bear
To punish for his faults this ever drunken sot,
With his Italian oaths? His is a happy lot.

OLIVER

He has fought much and well, been through some
 twenty wars.

NICOLE

Says so himself, no doubt!

OLIVER, *angrily*
                      Woman, I've seen his scars!
Merely a sight of him strikes terror all around
As with his martial tread his mailed foot spurns the
 ground.
He's our protector.

JACQUES

    Tcha! As oft I've said before,
All that protects us, sir, is the great castle door.

OLIVER, *angrily*

Silence!
(JACQUES *makes as though he would go on arguing*)
    Be still, I say! I and your master know
We have a hundred men in one in Vulcano.

NICOLE

If he's a hundred men, why are we always sent
With him when he's on guard, on to the battlement
To play at soldiers? (*Imitating*) March! pacing to left and right,
Carrying pikes by day, torches and lamps at night.
Why, too, unless to seem double our numbers, do
You make us all not one pike or torch bear, but two?
Surely your paladin, if he be worth a score
Of men-at-arms, on guard can have no need of more!

OLIVER

Where, now, is Vulcano? In the watch-tower?

JACQUES

                    Ho!
Down in the cellar.

ACT FIRST

OLIVER, *startled*
Why? What there does Vulcano?

JACQUES, *grinning*
He said he'd gone to drink all the sad thoughts away
Which had been troubling him since he had drawn no pay;
Said that to dry his eyes of their regretful brine,
As he could draw no pay, he'd go and draw your wine.

OLIVER, *startled*
Drinking! But Vulcano, when drunk, is mad, and takes
No care of what he does, whom he hurts, what he breaks.
We must be quiet, friends, try not to rouse him, for
Like a wild beast aroused from his lair, through that door
He would come storming up.

(JACQUES, NICOLE, *and the others exchange a look of intelligence, and all shout together at the top of their voices*)

JACQUES, NICOLE, JULIAN, *and* PIERRE
Pay us our wages!

OLIVER

Oh!
Softly, my friends, I beg!
(*In a panic*) Ah! Here is Vulcano!
I'll to the Baron! (*He runs off*)

PIERRE

There! Master will come, now, too!
He will be angry and—

JACQUES

Coward! Here's a to-do.
Lady Solange will come, too, on her father's arm.

NICOLE

Yes! And she will not let us poor folk come to harm.

JULIAN

No. She is sweet and kind.

PIERRE

Yes, but in case you know—

NICOLE

Here is the Baron! She's not with him.

JACQUES

Let us go!

(*All run out together. Enter the* BARON DE MAUT-PRÉ *and* OLIVER)

ACT FIRST

MAUTPRÉ

As long as Vulcano lies sleeping down below,
The others will not dare to brave us, will they?

OLIVER

No.

But how I wish, my lord, we dared a little more,
Dared rid us of this great braggart who irks us sore,
This long Italian, this—

MAUTPRÉ, *with some impatience*

Aye! But I fain would know
What is due to the men, and what to Vulcano.

OLIVER

To the men and Nicole eighteen months, if not more,
Eighteen months and some weeks.

MAUTPRÉ

To the Italian?

OLIVER

Four.

MAUTPRÉ

Twenty-two months in all. And what can we afford
To pay them in hard cash?

OLIVER

Nothing at all, my lord.

MAUTPRÉ

Good. Do not look surprised. The matter stands
   this way:
Nothing at all we have, so nothing can we pay;
Had we a little we half could pay and half owe,
Could satisfy the men and enrage Vulcano,
Or the Italian pay, and — there it is again —
By paying him alone enrage our honest men.
Therefore as it is clear with cash we cannot pay,
We fain, my Oliver, must find another way.

OLIVER

Another way, my lord, we fain must find. But still
I know of naught but cash an empty purse to fill.

MAUTPRÉ

And what is speech made for? I have seen dying
   men
At a mere spoken word rise up and fight again.
I have seen hungry men with a word sated be,
Angry men calmed, and calm men rise up angrily.
Speech is more than mere coin fitted the heart to
   reach.
We have no money, friend, but we have gift of
   speech,
And with the gift of speech I possess you shall see
This small household revolt finish quite peacefully.

ACT FIRST

OLIVER

What will you tell them?

MAUTPRÉ

I shall, when they come, unfold
The tale of swift alarms, quick flight, and hidden gold,
Which, as you know, maintains that treasure will be found
On the de Mautpré lands buried deep in the ground.

OLIVER

But is the legend true?

MAUTPRÉ, *with dignity*

That, sir, I do not know.
But I am very sure they will believe it so.
Summon them, nothing else can I devise to do.

OLIVER, *at the door*

Jacques, Nicole, Julian, Pierre, my lord would speak with you!

Enter JACQUES, PIERRE, JULIAN, NICOLE. *All are in evident fear of the* BARON, *and dare not speak*

MAUTPRÉ

Now then! What do you want? Will no one say the word?

JULIAN

Nothing, sir.

MAUTPRÉ

Nothing?

PIERRE

No, nothing at all, my lord.

JACQUES

Nothing, that is, except—

NICOLE, *desperately*

Nothing except our pay.

(*The* BARON *makes an angry gesture*)

JACQUES

Oh! not at once, my lord. When it may suit, some day.

MAUTPRÉ, *to* OLIVER *in feigned surprise*

Are they not paid?

OLIVER

My lord, not since December last.

NICOLE

Not since October, sir.

MAUTPRÉ

Ah! How the time has passed! Well! you shall all be paid; but, as you have been told,

ACT FIRST

Farm rents are due, and I at present have no gold.
No gold at hand, that is, for if I knew but where,
On my land, chests of gold, jewels beyond compare,
Lie waiting for me which centuries three ago
Hector de Mautpré hid, as you all doubtless know.

NICOLE

Nay, my lord, we know naught.

MAUTPRÉ

               Listen then. One dark night
Rose from the farms down there one long scream
  of affright
Out of the darkness, and, stricken with swift alarm,
Women and men rushed out, out of each house and
  farm,
Up to the castle gates, and made the night air
  ring
With their cries: "Help, my lord! Save us, my lord!
  The King!"
For those days, you must know, were not the days
  of peace,
And the King, fearing that Mautpré's wealth would
  increase
Until my ancestor should grasp the regal pow'r,
Had sent his soldiers down. Mautpré, within the
  hour,

Mustered his men within, calmed all the fear without,
Formed a great army, put the King's armed men to rout,
And, lest they should return, buried his treasure deep
Down in a sheltered spot under the castle keep.
Just where that treasure lies, no man has ever found,
But I know that it lies somewhere below the ground.
Treasure of coinèd gold, jewels beyond compare,
In mighty chests, brassbound, for me lie waiting there.
Soon we shall dig them up —
(*With sudden fierceness he turns on the servants who shrink before it*)

                      Now, sirs! The truth ye know,
Know that you will be paid. Why are you waiting? Go!
(*They huddle together and make for the door.* MAUTPRÉ *turns to* OLIVER)
It was not hard to stem the storm of discontent
With a few words, you see, spoken with that intent.

OLIVER

Aye, but the treasure?

ACT FIRST

MAUTPRÉ, *laughing*
>That, till it is found, will sleep
And be food for their dreams down there below the keep.
(*A tremendous uproar is heard from the cellar below*)
Beshrew my ears! What's that?

OLIVER
>It came up from below!

NICOLE, *peeping down the cellar stairs*
Oh! let us fly! He's drunk!

JACQUES
>Or mad!

OLIVER
>Who?

JACQUES
>Vulcano!

(VULCANO, *noisily drunk, staggers on to the stage through the little door leading to the cellar stairs, and, leaning against a pillar, looks around him at the* BARON, OLIVER, *and the servants*)

MAUTPRÉ
Whence come you, sirrah! Why such a wild air? Explain!

THE JESTERS

VULCANO

I come from death.

MAUTPRÉ, *coldly*
Indeed?

OLIVER, *aside*
Would he were back again!

VULCANO
with abundant gesture, exciting himself as he goes on
Aye, sirs, I come from death. Down in the cellar there
From my sleep I awoke. A blast of icy air
Circled me. 'Twas the cloak of a gigantic form,
Clad in a coat of mail. Out of the freezing storm
Circling it, it advanced, threat'ning, without a word.
I stood back to the wall, and sirs,
(*Slowly, solemnly, and with drunken emphasis*)
I drew my sword,
(*Suiting the action to the words*)
Cut and thrust! Whoop! Sa, ha! I advanced. He retired,
Thrust in carte, point, and tierce, eye nor wrist neither tired.
For a full hour we fought in the dark there below,
Till with both hands he dealt me such a mighty blow

ACT FIRST

Full on the sconce, that I staggered and with both hands
Clung to a pillar. (*Showing his hands*) See! These were as iron bands.
I was a Samson, for down came the pillar tall,
And I, my lord, came up to you here in the hall,
For 't was an omen! I came to relate the curse
Which must fall on Mautpré out of my empty purse!

MAUTPRÉ

How prick this windbag?

OLIVER

Hush! He's drunk, my lord. Beware!

VULCANO

Daggers and swords! I stand! Oliver, hand a chair!
(OLIVER *does so in spite of the* BARON's *annoyance*)
Ah! I'm athirst!

MAUTPRÉ

Again! Nay, sir, you've drunk enough.

(OLIVER *takes beaker and goblet from table*)

VULCANO, *with dignity*

I thirst, sir, for respect, not for the weakling stuff
Which you miscall your wine. Aye! and I'll have it too,

Or I (*he goes to the pillar*) will pull your walls down
 on the top of you.
Nay, never sneer! Enough! I am awrath today!
Give me the gold you owe, or by the saints—
(*He raises his sword*)

OLIVER

Nay, nay!
No bloodshed, Vulcano!
 (*He hands him a purse*) Here is your guerdon.
(*To the* BARON) I
Give him eight golden crowns, money I had put by
Last week for stores of food.

JACQUES, *to the other servants*

See! They're afraid!
(*Aloud*) And *we!*
Where is *our* pay?

VULCANO, *turning fiercely*
What now? That will come presently,
Next week, next month, next year—

JACQUES

But we—

VULCANO

I'll grind the bone
Into dust of the man who dares to raise his tone.

ACT FIRST

NICOLE

But our good gold!

VULCANO

Be still! Form up in line there! So!
Who are ye dare mistrust the word of Vulcano!
Baron, pray understand, not your gold did prevail
Against my anger. Naught but respect could avail.
Now then! Your halberds, quick! Strange are a man's affairs, —
I, Vulcano, command a regiment of hares!

(VULCANO *arms the three men and* NICOLE *with two halberds and a helmet apiece, and forms them into line. Plenty of comic business may be introduced here*)

VULCANO

By the right, march!

NICOLE

Oh! Oh! Pierre, you are joggling me!

VULCANO

Silence! Per Bacco! Now! By your right, one, two, three!
Up the stairs, and so, out! I follow last of all.
March! One, two, three! And out on to the castle wall!

NICOLE

I am afraid; my heart for very fear is sore,
What can a woman do under arms?

VULCANO

Make one more!
Forward—March!

(*Exeunt the four servants and* VULCANO *up the stairs leading to the battlements*)

OLIVER

God be thanked that they are gone at last!
Some good is Vulcano! There's one more danger past.

MAUTPRÉ

Now will I hie me back to my account books. You,
Oliver, try to fell just one more tree or two.

SOLANGE

who has entered just in time to hear this last order
Poor trees!

MAUTPRÉ

Solange!

SOLANGE

I heard sounds of strife here, methought.

MAUTPRÉ, *carelessly*

Our servant Vulcano had not done what he ought.
Well, I must go.

ACT FIRST

SOLANGE

My lord —

MAUTPRÉ

My child?

SOLANGE

'T was in my mind
To ask a boon, but —

MAUTPRÉ, *smiling*
But?

SOLANGE

I can no courage find.

MAUTPRÉ, *uneasily*

Boons mean expense.

OLIVER, *aside*

Poor child; I fear her slightest whim,
Cost what it may, will cost much, too much far, for him.

SOLANGE

Nay, father, 't will cost naught. But I do long to hear
News of the feast to which, by our next neighbour dear,
We were bid yesterday. There are to be, I'm told,

Sorcerers there, a witch, a tourney for the bold
Knights of the neighbourhood. Oh! I'm afire to go.
I must prepare me, sire. How did you answer?

MAUTPRÉ

No!

SOLANGE

Father! You have refused?

MAUTPRÉ

Yes, my child. You forget
Your tender years, my girl; the time has not come
yet
For jousts and tourneys.

SOLANGE

But—

MAUTPRÉ, *crossly*

I have said "no." Enough.
Let me hear naught again of tourneys and such
stuff.

(*Exit* MAUTPRÉ. OLIVER *looks curiously at* SO-
LANGE, *who, after a moment, bursts into tears*)

SOLANGE

Let us seek, Oliver. Perchance we two may find
Why, loving me, my lord is sometimes so unkind.

ACT FIRST

OLIVER

Nay, not unkind, my child; you are but seventeen.

SOLANGE

Old enough that, old friend, of jousts to be the queen.
No, there is something else; 'tis my heart tells me so.
Father's eyes shouted "yes" while his lips muttered "no."
Why, knowing as he knew what joy consent would give,
Did he of that delight his little girl deprive?

OLIVER

Now, now, you know full well—

SOLANGE

    Oliver, I believe
My second father, too, would his Solange deceive.
There are tears in your eyes because my eyes are dim;
Father's eyes, too, were moist when I looked up at him.
What does it mean?

  OLIVER, *affected*
  My child!

  SOLANGE, *nestling to him*
    Whisper that once again

Down in your heart, then say if you would give me pain.
Since mother went to rest in paradise above,
From you I've had, dear friend, almost a mother's love.
You fondled me, and with your finger in my hand
I learned to walk and run when I had learned to stand.
And once when, fever-rid, I tossed upon my bed,
You, Oliver, sat by, cooling my aching head,
Whispering gentle words, scolding in accents mild,
Chafing the icy feet of a small suff'ring child.
To make me laugh how oft on all fours you would crawl;
With you I first went out on to the castle wall;
You have enjoyed my joys, sorrowed at my distress,
And in my prison have brightened my loneliness.

OLIVER

Loneliness? Prison?

SOLANGE

              Aye. I am no baby now.
Why should my father not, like other sires, allow
Me some slight freedom? Why? Why should I lonely brood
Here in this castle's grim, unfriendly solitude?

ACT FIRST

OLIVER, *reproachfully*

Solitude?

SOLANGE

Oliver, do you remember how
Over a year ago, just eighteen months 't is now,
We wandered, you and I, down a tree-vaulted glade
In the wood, towards the brook, old man and little maid?
All was asleep. The leaves upon the trees were still,
The flowers slumbered each with curled bent head. The hill
Rose in the calm of sleep over the valley, glowed
Green, tipped with gold sunlight. Even the pale white road,
Dust-laden, slept in peace; for the wind slumbered, and
The brook's wee wavelets sang songs of a far dreamland.
All the birds sweetly slept, each in its feathered nest.
Nature was hushed, was taking her well-earnèd rest
After the storm of winter. Then with gentle thrill,
Nature awoke and stirred. The grass-blades on the hill
Stretched themselves in the sunshine, and with quiv'ring gleam

The sun replied, awoke, warmed with its darting beam
The green tree vault above. The breeze awoke, and strong
With its first waking sang, tempting the brook to song.
All the birds answered; sang to their friends, wind and sun,
Sang the glad hymn of life, merging it ev'ry one
Into the birds' love-song. In my heart something stirred,
Fluttered, awoke, and lived, sung to life by the bird!
Something which must awake in ev'ry maiden's breast,
Something which changes peace into a sweet unrest,
Something which, craving, pleads for a gift from above,
Something which whispers her that God's great gift is love.
My eyes were wet, my heart throbbed, and I seemed to fear
Nature's glad message now, after the winter drear;
But as the wavelets danced and as the sunlight beamed,
Warmer and warmer a voice from the sunlight seemed

ACT FIRST

To raise its hymn of joy, and in glad tones to sing:
"Maid, thou art woman now! Waken! Here is the
 spring!"
I have no words to tell what I would fain explain,
Old friend, but do not let me sink to sleep again.
Try, dear, to understand, strive what I mean to find,
Without plain words. I know your heart will help
 your mind.
Old friend, your child's heart craves for something
 all unknown,
Which the sunbeams told her springs from the good
 God's throne.
Help me, dear friend, to find it.

>OLIVER, *much moved, but with a half smile*
>>If I help in this,
What guerdon shall be mine?

>SOLANGE, *throwing her arms around his neck*
>>A loving daughter's kiss.

>OLIVER, *half to himself, half to* SOLANGE
So then I too have slept, and the weight of my years
Crushed down the old man's pow'r to see a young
 girl's tears.
Now my heart is awake, it cannot yet rejoice,
For from above it drop tears in your mother's voice,
Softly reproaching. So, wiseacre deaf and blind,

I have been erring. Not trying the truth to find,
Satisfied with the lore musty old books have given,
On parchment peering down instead of up to heaven,
Wise in the bookworm's lore, by other fools compiled,
Knowing the world, ignoring your true heart, my child,
Reading the stars, not seeing life's true guerdon lay
Not in the starlit night, but in the sunlit day.
Child, can you now forgive? See, I my sin confess,
And will in future strive to win your happiness.

SOLANGE

No pardon, dear, you need — old men are ever so;
They search and seek for things which younger hearts all know,
Searching, they cannot find. It is the human lot.
What in a young heart glows is by old hearts forgot.
Dear one, you do not know —

OLIVER

                                     Aye, from today I do,
And having always loved, know you and love you too;
And as your heart forgives thoughtlessly given pain,
Now that we know, we are, I hope, old friends again.

ACT FIRST

SOLANGE, *gaily*

Answer my question then. Why does my father now,
When I would dance, refuse? Why with deep-wrinkled brow,
Grudging himself the joy to see me glad, does he
Keep me within these walls alone, unceasingly?
Every "no" he speaks pains him. I read his eyes
As you read books, and see. Why then this sacrifice?
Why does he grudge me joy? Why make my young heart sore?
Punishing me, I know, punishes him yet more.

OLIVER

Dear heart, the reason is, Mautpré is passing poor.
Poverty is the cause of your fast-closèd door,
For on your father's back ever together ride
Two grim, unsparing guests, poverty and his pride.

SOLANGE

Poverty?

OLIVER

Aye.

SOLANGE

Poor sire! Why did I never know?

OLIVER

'T is his wish. Never let him guess I told you so.

SOLANGE

Nay, of course, by no word.

Enter the BARON DE MAUTPRÉ *with a paper in his hand*

OLIVER

Hush!

MAUTPRÉ

Here upon this plan
I have marked woods to fell. Oliver, look, my man.
(*Sees* SOLANGE) Still here, Solange?

SOLANGE

Yes, father, I've been scolded so
By Oliver, and wait for your forgiveness.

MAUTPRÉ, *smiling*

Oh,
You are forgiven, sweet; you cannot plead in vain
For pardon. Do not let it, though, occur again.

OLIVER, *who has been looking at the plan*
Yes. This will bring in gold, and —

MAUTPRÉ, *quickly, with a glance at* SOLANGE
'T will improve the view
From the east window.

ACT FIRST

SOLANGE

    Sirs, I bid good day to you.
I have my household cares, my dove to feed.
(*She curtsies and trips up the staircase and out*)

MAUTPRÉ, *to* OLIVER, *poring over the plan*
          You see
Twelve cords from Coulange glade,—good wood,
 too, they tell me,—
Fifteen at Valvert, twelve —

VULCANO, *bursting into the room*
        Up to the gate there ride
Three evil-looking men, each on a mule astride.

MAUTPRÉ

Spies again, doubtless!

VULCANO, *staggering*
       Fear not; my men are below.
I go to join them!
(*Menacingly shaking his sword at the window*)
    Ah! Scoundrels! You're doomed, I trow.
(*He goes towards the door and is met by* JACQUES)

JACQUES

Good my lord, 't is three pedlars would have au-
 dience, they

Have with them things of worth and of virtu,
   they say.

VULCANO

Pedlars, are they? Aha! So they escape my sword.
Had they been thieves, I would —

MAUTPRÉ, *handing him a paper*

Vulcano, send this word
With all speed to the town.
(*To* JACQUES) Bring in the pedlars. I
Will see their wares. (*Exit* JACQUES)
(*To* OLIVER) We may look, though we cannot buy.

(JACQUES *shows in an old pedlar, who is followed by*
RENÉ DE CHANCENAC *and* ROBERT DE BEL-
FONTE, *disguised as porters and carrying large
packs*)

PEDLAR

God keep you, sirs.

OLIVER *and* MAUTPRÉ
And you.

MAUTPRÉ, *looking at* PEDLAR
Do I not know your face?

PEDLAR

Étienne, from Elbœuf town, an it so please your
   grace.

ACT FIRST

MAUTPRÉ

Ah, yes. And so you've something I may buy, Étienne?
Well, well, undo your packs for me.
(*With sudden suspicion*) Who are those men?

PEDLAR, *in some confusion*

Good my lord, porters both.

MAUTPRÉ

Men I've not seen before.

PEDLAR

No, my lord. Lately hired.

MAUTPRÉ, *to* RENÉ *and* ROBERT

Friends, wait outside the door.
(*To* OLIVER) They spy around too much.

PEDLAR

But good my lord!

MAUTPRÉ

How so!

Gave I no order, sir?

PEDLAR

Good my lord—

OLIVER

Bid them go!

(PEDLAR *makes a sign to* RENÉ *and* ROBERT, *who go out*)

MAUTPRÉ

Now what have you to show?

PEDLAR, *kneeling, to undo his packs*
             Sirs, I've new things and old,
Armour, steel corselets, spears, daggers, and cloth of gold;
Velvet from Venice.

MAUTPRÉ
      No. These do not please me.

PEDLAR
                      Well,
If you care not to buy, sir, have you naught to sell?

MAUTPRÉ, *interested, with a glance at* OLIVER
Sell? Some oddments, perhaps, to sell I have a mind.
I'll go and see. Wait here. Oliver, we might find
One or two things.

(*Exit* BARON *in converse with* OLIVER. *The* PEDLAR, *on tiptoe, calls in* RENÉ *and* ROBERT)

RENÉ
     Beshrew me! So a Chancenac waits
At the door.

ROBERT, *loudly*
De Belfonte—

ACT FIRST

PEDLAR, *imploring a quieter tone*
>When, at the castle gates,

I begged you'd show discretion, you both promised.

RENÉ
>True.

But we did not expect—

PEDLAR
>What would you have me do?

I'm but a pedlar, you are for the day my men;
If you but raise your voice, out we all go again.

RENÉ, *looking round him*
Poverty reigns, I see. So it is true what I
Was told about Mautpré's odd eccentricity.

PEDLAR
Lower, my lord, your presence here is an outrage.

ROBERT, *laughing*
>No!

'T is to decide a bet. Did we not tell you so?
René, against all sense, maintains that wit ensnares
A maiden's heart.

RENÉ
>Belfonte, fatuous fool, declares

That a man's beauty o'er a man's wit will prevail,

And that where wit may win, a handsome face may fail.

####### ROBERT

Yes! And to prove our points—

####### RENÉ

           We had to find the maid.
There is one here, Étienne; but be not you afraid:
We'll be discreet. Mautpré shall not know our intent.

####### ROBERT, *laughing*

No; lest he call his men down from the battlement.
'T is Oliver must help. With this old friend of mine
And of my father's, we will some sage plan combine
To gain us entry here.

####### RENÉ, *laughing*

           On this side of the door.

####### PEDLAR

I hear them coming back. Pray ye, sweet lords, no more.

(*He pushes them out. Enter* DE MAUTPRÉ, *followed by* OLIVER *and* JACQUES)

####### MAUTPRÉ, *to the* PEDLAR

We've found some things below, if you will come with me.

ACT FIRST

PEDLAR

Have you no suits of mail, cuirass for cavalry,
Spurs, daggers, gorgets, or —

MAUTPRÉ

Aye, there's my martial gear,
Helmet, spurs, all complete. Go, Jacques, and bring
it here. (*Exit* JACQUES)
There is the stout cuirass which, in the Pavian strife,
Won me the royal thanks in that it saved my life.

PEDLAR

Good!

MAUTPRÉ

You must pay it dear, for 'twas a valued friend,
In fifteen twenty-five, when stout blows without end
Rained down on it. Ah, me! Those were heroic days,
And I fought hard to win my royal master's praise.
Each time my blade I swung, a Spaniard bit the dust;
But the blade has been cleaned and is quite free from rust.
And the blows I received my good cuirass did scorn,
For 'tis of finest steel.

JACQUES, *bringing in coat of armour*

It has not yet been worn,
And is in perfect state.

PEDLAR, *coughing to hide his amusement*
   Hem! hum!

MAUTPRÉ, *to* JACQUES
    You idiot!
     (*To* PEDLAR) He
Must be excused, Étienne; he knows no history.
On the bright surface each blow once could be seen
 —here!
Here again! The repairs cost me exceeding dear.

PEDLAR, *who has been examining the suit*
On the back here's a dent.

MAUTPRÉ
    On the back? Let me look.
(*With offended dignity*)
'Tis here we hang it up. 'Tis the mark of the hook.

PEDLAR
What will you take for it?

OLIVER
    'Tis priceless, for't has borne
The brunt of battle and was by a hero worn.

MAUTPRÉ
How would you price, Étienne, great Hector's shield and spear?

ACT FIRST

How can I price the suit of armour that is here?
Shall I say eighty crowns? A hundred? I know not.

PEDLAR

Say forty and I buy.

MAUTPRÉ

   Nay, sirrah! Why, God wot,
I do not care to sell.

PEDLAR
Sixty crowns.

OLIVER, *to* DE MAUTPRÉ

     Let it go.
We need the gold. He may buy other things below.

MAUTPRÉ

Take it then.

PEDLAR, *counting and paying*
Sixty crowns.

MAUTPRÉ

    Oliver, take his gold.
Now come with me and price a brass-bound chest.
 'Tis old
Oaken, wondrously carved; from an old abbey torn,
Where it held treasure.

PEDLAR
  Now in it you store—

MAUTPRÉ

Our corn.

(MAUTPRÉ *and the* PEDLAR *go out. Enter* ROBERT *and* RENÉ, *who have been peeping in, waiting until* OLIVER *was alone*)

OLIVER, *putting away the money*
Sixty gold crowns in hand.—Robert de Belfonte!

ROBERT

I
Would have your pardon for coming thus privily,
But, friend, in you I trust. I know you wish me well.
I and de Chancenac here (OLIVER *bows*) have an odd tale to tell.

RENÉ, *bowing*
Odd? No! The old, old tale youth ever tells to age.
We are in love.

OLIVER
In love?

ROBERT
You were my grandsire's page,
And with my father made vow of true friendship.
Now
I, sir, my father's son, ask you to keep that vow.

ACT FIRST

OLIVER

In love?

RENÉ

With sweet Solange. Nay, start not. Not one word
From our lips of our love has that sweet maiden heard.
As the bird which she fed when we first saw her, she,
Sweet Solange de Mautpré, from all offence is free.

OLIVER, *looking from one to another*
In love? And with Solange? Both of you?

ROBERT

       Hear our tale.
And I am sure your heart's true kindness will prevail
Over all prejudice. 'Tis but a week agone,
In mind and heart my friend René and I were one.
Then we both saw the maid, and now we drift apart,
For her sweet picture fills all of my —

RENÉ

       And my heart.
Help us, good sir. 'Tis time two old friends were at peace,
Time that strife between two brothers in arms should cease.
Both of us love the maid —

OLIVER

Love her, young sir, but how?
You say you've seen her. Where? How can you love her now?

RENÉ

Shooting, one day, the birds drew us near to the line
Which, as you know, divides de Mautpré's lands from mine,
And, through a quickset hedge, our thoughts of aught but love,
We saw the fair Solange feeding a milk-white dove.
It kissed her lips, her neck, rippled her golden hair
With its pink beak. To me, standing and gazing there,
It was as though some saint touching my sinful eyes
Had granted them a glance into God's Paradise.

ROBERT

I too could scarce believe Solange was not divine,
And, like René, felt straight that I must make her mine.
What now to do?

OLIVER, *to himself as much as to the young men*

'Tis true. Little Solange must wed,
Seventeen years have passed over her golden head.
But if I help the child these two fair youths to see,

ACT FIRST

Will not Mautpré with right say I act trait'rously?
And if I help her not, do not I wrong her sore?
De Mautpré owes me much. I owe Solange far more.
Sirs, I will serve your wish. To that I pledge my troth.
(*Aside*) God grant that serving them I may be serving both
De Mautpré and Solange.

ROBERT

     Let us a plan devise
By which we both may be seen by the dainty prize
Each of us hopes to win.

OLIVER

     It will be hard to find,
For dark suspicion lurks deep in de Mautpré's mind.
Poverty's pride forbids his oldest friends the door,
Lest coming they should see that he is now grown poor.
Yet will I think.

RENÉ

    And when we may return again,
Send word to me.

ROBERT

Or me.

RENÉ, *laughing*

    Send, if you can, two men,
Each with the one word "Come."

OLIVER

    Well, I will not say no.
But now, my young friends both, the word I say is "Go."
You've tarried long enough.

RENÉ

    Hush! Here the maiden comes.

ROBERT, *jealously*

How know you that, René?

RENÉ, *with a smile*

    A pricking in my thumbs.

(SOLANGE *appears in the gallery carrying her white dove in a cage*)

SOLANGE, *to her dove*

Each day, well in the shade, my bird, I hang your cage.
Why, then, in your plump breast does fruitless anger rage,
Ruffling it with the sound of a weak old man's snore?
Know you not, foolish bird, if through your open door

ACT FIRST

I let you fly, your life would be the forfeit? Aye,
All the wild birds would peck and mock you as you
 die.
Evil aye stalks abroad. But do not be afraid,
Cages there always are for each young bird—(*a
 little sadly*) or maid.
(*She hangs her cage up on the branch of a climbing
rose-tree;* ROBERT, RENÉ, *and* OLIVER *stand watching her*)

RENÉ

She is delicious.

ROBERT

  Yes.

RENÉ

    She lends these crumbling walls
All the poetic sheen of the enchanted halls
Of the old legends. See the light upon her head
As she hangs up her cage. Did you hear what she
 said
To the white bird? I fear, Robert, we wrong her. Oh,
Let us forego our bet!

ROBERT

    Double it rather! No?
Does "ready wit" now fear that it will meet rebuff?
Are you afraid to lose, that you hold back?

RENÉ

Enough!

(*To* OLIVER) On you we count, sir.

SOLANGE

speaking to the bird and coming down stage (*the young men stand back*)

There! coo to the sun and look
Out to the farms, while I, diligent, con my book.

OLIVER

Peste! I can think of naught! What is your book, my child?

SOLANGE

'T is John the Jester's tale, who, by his capers wild,
Gladdened King Philip's court until in love he fell.
(*Pensively*) A jester here would make, were we but rich —

OLIVER

Ah, well,

That may come.

SOLANGE

Which? The jester or —

OLIVER, *aside*

I have my plan.

(*To* SOLANGE) Both perhaps. But now, hark!
Just to please an old man,

ACT FIRST

When Mautpré comes, be still or speak of languor, and
When he is looking, lean your fair head on your hand.
I have no time to tell you why. 'T is but a trap
Into which a sunbeam may find its way, mayhap.

Enter MAUTPRÉ *and* VULCANO

MAUTPRÉ

Oliver, what is wrong? More woeful tales to tell,
Needing another sale?

OLIVER, *pointing to* SOLANGE
                      Hush, sir, she is not well.

MAUTPRÉ

Not well?

OLIVER

  No, good my lord. Too long this castle drear
Has cloistered her. To me her case is sadly clear.
Her languor—

MAUTPRÉ, *kneeling by her chair*
           My Solange, have I neglected you?

SOLANGE

playing the part OLIVER *has bidden her to play*
No, father, no, I cast no jot of blame on you,
But if I could but laugh, nay, if I could but smile,

If some one could my life's sad moments but beguile!

MAUTPRÉ, *despairingly*

Oliver, you're a leech!

OLIVER

What says Hippocrates
In his immortal book on melancholy? These
Are cases which to cure no drugs we should apply,
But look to jesters rather for our remedy.

MAUTPRÉ

To jesters?

SOLANGE

Jesters?

OLIVER

Yes.

VULCANO

Rich lords keep one or two.
Their tricks are much like those which dogs or monkeys do.

OLIVER

They animate a court and might amuse our dear.

MAUTPRÉ

A jester by all means! How can we get one here?
How are you now, Solange?

ACT FIRST

SOLANGE

          Better, I think, my lord.
Be not distressed.

MAUTPRÉ

          But how to spread abroad the word
That we a jester need?

Enter PEDLAR, *followed by* ROBERT *and* RENÉ

PEDLAR

          Now, my men, pray ye do
Get to work; fasten up these three packs, both of you!

OLIVER, *aside to the young men*

Listen! My plan is found.

(*To the* BARON) Good my lord, by your grace,
I will indite the scroll which shall, from place to place,
In all the villages from Mautpré down to Tours,
In ev'ry market-place tell all this need of yours.
(*He sits and writes, reading aloud what he is writing.*)
"Wanted, a jester whose converse can entertain
A maid of high degree, and make her smile again;
A jester of rare wit, courtly, refined, and
Trustworthy"—

ROBERT, *aside to* RENÉ

          What is this?

RENÉ

　　Hush, man, I understand.

CURTAIN

As the curtain (a slow one) descends, RENÉ *and* ROBERT *load the packs on to their shoulders.*

THE SECOND ACT

ACT SECOND

The great reception room of the Château de Maut-pré. This great baronial hall shows many signs of dilapidation, but many, also, of its glories in the past. A large window (up stage) affords a magnificent view over the country-side. The room is being trimmed with garlands of wild flowers so disposed as to hide the mural dilapidations wherever possible. A large state armchair with a smaller seat beside it have been placed for DE MAUTPRÉ *and* SOLANGE. *Opposite these seats, and somewhat to one side, is a wooden bench. As the curtain rises* VULCANO *is superintending the work of* JACQUES, *of* JULIAN, *and of* PIERRE *who are hanging the garlands.*

VULCANO

Hang that piece higher—No. Somewhat more to
 the left,
Now to the right. Dio! Of eyesight art bereft?
Drop the loop of your wreath. Not so much, dolt.
 Stop! There!
So shall we have a hall bedecked beyond compare
With all your tapestries panelled or set in frieze.
Nowhere, embroidered, shall you find such flow'rs
 as these.

What is that scarlet flow'r which twinkles like a star
Up there?

JACQUES

'Tis pimpernel.

VULCANO

And those green ones which are
So lightly graceful there? Say, sirrah, what are they?

JACQUES

Those? They are hops, i' faith—you see them ev'ry day.

VULCANO

'T is well. Clear up the mess of moss and fallen leaves,
That when the baron comes he naught of it perceives.
Dress yourselves in your best and when dressed come below.

(*As they go out by one door,* OLIVER *enters by another and sees the decorations*)

OLIVER

Artist, I see, as well as fighter, Vulcano.

VULCANO

Pooh! An idea of mine. Still I admit to you
My garlands do look well hung thus.

ACT SECOND

OLIVER

Indeed they do.
'T is pleasant, too, to think that all these tapestries
So charmingly arranged, so pleasant to the eyes,
Cost naught.

VULCANO

That is because I know with half an eye
How I can make the most of such field mercery
As pimpernel and hops —

OLIVER

How many jesters, pray,
Are there in waiting?

VULCANO

Three of them have come to-day.
They are but sorry knaves. In the guard-room they sit,
And not one of the three appears to have much wit.

OLIVER, *to himself, anxiously*

Where are the two young lords, who promised they would come,
For whom this tourney was proclaimed with beat of drum?
Were they but jesting? No. They plan some glad surprise.
(*Aloud*) Comes no one? Vulcano! You have the better eyes,

Look down the road. No fools you see who wend
  their ways
Up to the castle?

>   VULCANO, *at window*
>   >   One. (OLIVER *runs to window*)
>   >   >   Our ass was set to graze
By the road.

>   OLIVER
>   >   Imbecile. Ah! Here comes de Mautpré!
Show him your garlands, then go watch the king's
  highway
In case more jesters come.

>   *Enter* MAUTPRÉ

>   MAUTPRÉ
>   >   Bravo, my friends, bravo!
How brave a show of flow'rs. Who made it?

>   OLIVER
>   >   >   Vulcano.

>   MAUTPRÉ
'Tis skilfully well done.

>   VULCANO
>   >   >   Florentines in their heart
Cherish a trinity of gods: love, war, and art.

ACT SECOND

MAUTPRÉ

None of those who may come to-day must even guess
That we are poor. Your flow'rs hide my poor walls'
   distress.
I thank you, Vulcano. (*To* OLIVER, *who is standing
by the window crossing himself devoutly and mur-
muring prayers*)
      Why, Oliver, what now?
Why these signs of the cross, devotion-wrinkled
   brow,
And mumbled prayers?

OLIVER, *in some confusion*
    Three! But three jesters are here,
Three to choose from, and if Solange we are to cheer
We must have more—five fools—two more at least
   —the three
Are far too few.

MAUTPRÉ, *carelessly*
    Unless one of those three be he
Whom we elect to keep. Tell me how does Nicole
In her duenna's dress fill her duenna's rôle?

OLIVER

Passing well, good my lord. Vows, tho', she cannot
   budge
In her corset of wood. But you yourself shall judge.

She waits without. Holà! Holà! Without, I say!

(*Throws open a door and announces with mock ceremony*)

Make way for Dame Nicole, duenna de Mautpré.

(NICOLE, *looking extremely uncomfortable in her grand clothes, comes in and is inspected by the* BARON)

MAUTPRÉ

How do you feel, Nicole, in these fine clothes?

NICOLE

My lord,
Like a fowl trussed to roast. Never, upon my word,
Have I been ill at ease as I am now. I seem
To be packed in a case. If it lasts I shall scream
Loud for help presently, thinking, my lord, that I
Have been encoffined now, living, before I die.
This ruff around my neck chokes me—I never could
Be a great dame and wear this great corset of wood.
(*She taps it*)
With it I cannot breathe; I cannot (*showing her dress*) walk in this
Bell-shaped thing, and my shoes are pointed miseries.
Give me back, good my lord, my rags of yesterday;
In these I feel, i'faith, a dressed-up ape.

ACT SECOND

MAUTPRÉ

Hey, hey!
Here's gratitude.

OLIVER

Come, come. 'Tis not so bad, I trow.
Show us the reverence I taught you. So! And now
Go fetch your mistress in. And do not drag your feet
As you walk. Lift them up. So! And let me entreat
You not to wipe your nose on your sleeve.

NICOLE

Well, but, sir,
What shall I wipe it on? My gloves, my stomacher?

MAUTPRÉ

Go now, and fetch Solange.

NICOLE

I go, my lord. This train
Will trip me up. I long to scrub my pans again
And wear my kitchen dress. In that at least I look
Not like a doll dressed up, but what I am—a cook.
(*She goes out*)

MAUTPRÉ

Now, Oliver, 'tis time. (*Pointing*) Post here the men-at-arms

With the ploughmen whom you have brought up
   from the farms;
The jesters on this bench. We, by this door in state,
Will make our entry — Too long do not let us wait.
(*He goes out*)

OLIVER

And all this for the two who have not come. I fear
(*shaking his head*)
None of the three we have will be your mate, my
   dear.
(*Opening guard-room door*) Now, Vulcano.

VULCANO

       Holà!

OLIVER

     Come in, and place your men.

(OLIVER *goes to the window. Enter from guard-
room* VULCANO *with* JACQUES, PIERRE, JULIAN,
*etc., etc. They are helmeted, dressed in breastplates
and buff jerkins, and armed with halberds which they
manage with some difficulty*)

JULIAN

Murder! Help! On my foot your lance-butt dropped
   again.

JACQUES

'Twas your own fault.

VULCANO

No more.

JACQUES

But he—

VULCANO

Maladetto!
Silence I say. Stand there. You there, and there. I know
(*To* JULIAN) You will put out an eye with your lance point.

JULIAN

Perchance
It would be no bad thing to take away my lance.

VULCANO

Rest on it, dolt. (*Calling*) Now, you fool triad, sit there, pray,
And forget not to rise when the lord of Mautpré
And his fair daughter come.

(*The three jesters,* HILARIUS, BAROCO, *and* JACK PUDDING, *enter and take their places on the bench.* HILARIUS, *white-faced, clean-shaven, and sinister looking, is dressed in black and scarlet and is in appearance the exact opposite of his name.* BAROCO *is a smirking, affected Italian, and* JACK PUDDING *is a grinning peasant lad*)

HILARIUS, *in a deep and mournful voice*
It is damp here.

> BAROCO, *looking round him*
> Is this the vaunted wealth of France?

JACK PUDDING

Heigho! Take care (*to* JULIAN), you'll put my eye out with your lance.

JULIAN

Whose fault is that but yours? Your thick head's in my way.

VULCANO

Way for the Baron George Charles Henry de Mautpré!

(*Enter* DE MAUTPRÉ *and* SOLANGE *hand in hand followed by* NICOLE *who carries* SOLANGE'S *handkerchief and fan. The* BARON *and* SOLANGE *sweep ceremoniously round towards their places, while the "men-at-arms" salute as best they can and the three jesters rise from their bench and bow deeply.* NICOLE, *who is anxious to sit down, plumps into the big state chair intended for her master, then, when he sees her, upon* SOLANGE'S *stool, and eventually takes her stand behind* SOLANGE. *At a sign from* VULCANO *the three jesters resume their seats*)

ACT SECOND

OLIVER

Does my lord condescend these men to interview?

(MAUTPRÉ *nods assent*)

VULCANO

Avanti, then, the first. Now, red face, up with you.

(JACK PUDDING *gets up and giggles foolishly*)

OLIVER, *aside*

They cannot mean to come.

MAUTPRÉ

Well, have you naught to say,
And if not, prithee, why have you come here to-day?

JACK PUDDING

My name is Pudding. (*All laugh*)

SOLANGE, *to* NICOLE

He is not ill-named. I had
No fitter name found.

NICOLE

But he is a likely lad.

JACK PUDDING, *after a pause*

My name is Pudding.

OLIVER

So you have already said.

JACK PUDDING, *another pause*

Pudding, my name is.

MAUTPRÉ, *smiling*

Or perhaps 'tis pudding-head.

(*All laugh as in duty bound at* DE MAUTPRÉ's *little joke*)

PUDDING

My name is Pudding. When last Monday the man came

And read his parchment, all the farm-hands said 'twere shame

If I did not obtain the fool's place speedily,

As none of them had seen a greater fool than I.

(*Everybody laughs at him*)

OLIVER

I doubt it not, my lad. Where have you served before?

PUDDING

Down on the farm, that's all. But that's no matter, for

I've always played the fool, little else did I do.

I always have amused the lads (*with a grin*) and lasses too.

MAUTPRÉ

We doubt not that all must have laughed at you, i'fegs.

ACT SECOND

SOLANGE

How did you make the lasses laugh?

PUDDING, *giggling loudly*

A' pinched their legs.

OLIVER, *to the* BARON

This Pudding shall I send at once back to his farm?
He is no good.

MAUTPRÉ

'Tis true. But he can do no harm.
Let him stay here his month.

VULCANO

prods BAROCO *with his sword. He springs into the
air and cuts a caper*

Your name, sir.

BAROCO

Baroco,
My name is, and that name you, my lord, doubtless know.
For ten years past that name has made all Florence
smile.

VULCANO

You are from Florence?

BAROCO

Si, signore.

VULCANO
>Wait a while.

From Florence? Italian? Why, yes! This man I
know.
Ecco la meraviglia. Come sta, Baroco?
Buon giorno, mio caro. Godo di vederla,
Baroco, come va la sua famiglia?

BAROCO
Per la grazia di Dio, sta bene tutta.

MAUTPRÉ, *who is tiring of this effusion*
>Do

Not, I pray, let your feelings overpower you.
Let us proceed.

VULCANO, *surprised*
>Proceed? Did I not say that I

Knew him, my lord? And that he comes from Italy?
Surely that is enough and these two fools may go.
No jester will you find better than Baroco.

OLIVER
Our lord must judge of that.

VULCANO
>Judge? But the man's my friend!

Surely my lord to me no insult can intend?

ACT SECOND

MAUTPRÉ, *to* BAROCO

Where have you served before?

(BAROCO *is much embarrassed and remains silent*)

VULCANO, *quickly*
      Baron de Polignac
Was his first master. Then the Duke of Lambrissac.

MAUTPRÉ

Well, we shall see. Now, you dressed all in sable, why
Being a jester do you dress so soberly?

(HILARIUS, *who is dressed in black from head to foot, with the exception of his belt and of the coxcomb on his black donkey's-eared cap, which are scarlet, rises to his feet. He is tall and thin, cadaverous of face, and looks anything but a merrymaker*)

HILARIUS, *in a hollow voice*
Hilarius my name and so my nature too.
Though I may not appear a joyful man to you,
Usually I am gay as the morning lark,
Singing and full of fun from early dawn till dark.
But I am sad just now; family woes insist
On a fool's hearing them, and I could not resist.
But, good my lord, this day of my grief is the last,

And you will find me gay when the dark cloud has passed.

OLIVER

Surely we do not need a jester who is sad.

SOLANGE

Poor fellow, let him stay.

MAUTPRÉ

Well, stay your month, my lad.
In a month from to-day my daughter will decide
Which of you shall remain.

VULCANO, *in a fury*

So you my choice deride.
I tell you, none there is better than Baroco,
But you forsooth will not hearken to Vulcano.
Maledetto! My lord, but you shall rue this sore.

OLIVER
who has been at the window, in great excitement

Heed him not, good my lord! My lord, here are two more.

MAUTPRÉ

Two?

OLIVER

Two more jesters who are knocking at the gate. (*To* JACQUES) Go down and let them in.

ACT SECOND

MAUTPRÉ

They have come somewhat late.

OLIVER

Forgive them, good my lord, they may come from afar,
And I believe these two far better jesters are
Than the three we have heard.

VULCANO

What proof have you of it?

OLIVER

My eyes convince me that these two are men of wit.

MAUTPRÉ

What say you, my Solange?

SOLANGE

I say, admit them. I
Feel that the one of them may cure my malady.

OLIVER

Here they are.

(*Enter* RENÉ *and* ROBERT. *They make low obeisance to the* BARON, SOLANGE, *and the company generally. Each of them wears a long cloak and neither wears cap and bells, but each has a little three-cornered hat*)

MAUTPRÉ

Sirs, 't is late.

RENÉ, *as* CHICOT

My lord, reproach us not.
Surely, an you will think on it, hard is our lot,
And we are punished sore in that so late we meet
Mentor with one of the three Graces at his feet.

(*There is a gentle hum of approval at the compliment*)

OLIVER

Cleverly turned. (*He rubs his hands*)

MAUTPRÉ, *to* OLIVER

This young man has a pretty wit.

OLIVER

I knew 't was so, my lord; I felt quite sure of it.

MAUTPRÉ

Well, sirs, as you are here, tell us your names and say
Each why you think to be jester to de Mautpré.

ROBERT, *as* NARCISSUS

Narcissus is my name, a name poets have sung;
On jest's step-ladder I have held the highest rung,
For to my wit the gods a precious gift have joined,
A gift worth more than all the gold was ever coined,
The gift of beauty. Wit alone is not enough.

ACT SECOND

The eye loves to drink in the beauties of a ruff
Well starched, of virgin white, and to rest on a man
Whose pourpoint clothes him well. My meaning, sir, I can
Prove in a moment. Who would choose an ugly knave
For servant just because he happened to be brave?
An ugly man in park or terrace to display
Blots out their loveliness, takes half their charm away.
It is not for their song or for their wit, sir, but
For their sheer beauty that the peacocks proudly strut
On castle terrace, parapet, and lawn, I trow,
And a poor jester's plea for beauty you'll allow
For the same reason. He, I think, should harmonize
With and set off each thing on which may rest your eyes,
Should of a faulty pillar e'en correct the line,
Should with his grace of wit a grace of form combine
To charm the senses, should be handsome, straight, and strong.
Apollo was the god of more than of mere song,
And, good my lord, I think a jester for his part
Should be worth gazing at, a living work of art,

And that he should not please by stringing words
  alone,
But, silent, please you more than beauty carved in
  stone.

(*He throws off his cloak, appearing in a well fitting
suit of rose-coloured silk. There is a murmur of admiration at his handsome figure*)

OLIVER

This young man will break hearts.

SOLANGE

      What grace he has!

NICOLE

        I' fegs,

A proper youth and what a proper pair of legs.

NARCISSUS

Who cares for wisdom which from ill-shaped lips one
  hears?
Our eyes have their rights just as surely as our ears.
A lovely pearl, well set, will ill-set pearls surpass,
Good wine has better taste out of a well-cut glass.
Can you imagine an Achilles with a limp,
A Paris in the shape of a deformèd imp?
And who would dare to limn Adonis with a leer
Unevenly absurd? Or Venus, drawing near
In dove-drawn carriage, thin and angular portray?

ACT SECOND

Beauty has equal worth, more worth than wit, I say.
Who would not rather far a love-bird listen to
Than to a grim gray parrot's hoarse-voiced speech?
  And you
Will bear me out in this, sweet lady, whose white dove
Is the incarnate shape of beauty and of love.
Well, I, Narcissus, am a love-bird and demand,
Wise sire and gentle maid, indulgence at your hand.

OLIVER
His speech is as well turned out as he is forsooth.

VULCANO
We summoned jesters here, not love-birds, dainty youth.

NARCISSUS, *looking* VULCANO *up and down*
At you, my scraggy friend, but once I need to gaze
To see why beauty's name your senses should amaze
And anger.

    VULCANO, *drawing his dagger*
      Cospetto!

    OLIVER, *holds up his arm*
          Stay. Jesters we permit
All license they desire and do but laugh at it.

They may say what they will. And therefore from this youth,
Brave Vulcano, you must for once accept—

NARCISSUS, *laughing*

The truth.

(VULCANO, *more furious than ever, makes a rush at* NARCISSUS, *but* OLIVER *and* BAROCO *hold him back*)

MAUTPRÉ, *to* VULCANO

Even at kings their fools such insolence have flung
That all save fools for such words had straightway been hung.
Charlemagne never raged when his fool teased him.

VULCANO
with immense dignity, sheathing his weapon

So?

If Charlemagne endured, I vengeance may forego.

SOLANGE, *to* OLIVER

He showed no fear.

OLIVER

This jester's proved himself a man.

MAUTPRÉ, *to* CHICOT

'Tis your turn now. Speak up and show us, if you can,

ACT SECOND

Your title and your claim our jester here to be.
Do your best. I admit Narcissus pleases me.

CHICOT, *advances and bows*
(*Speaking rapidly and with as much "zip" as can be got into the delivery of each verse*)

You all, of course, should know my name,
My qualities you ought to guess,
But time will teach you them and frame
My memory in gold, unless
I please you not, when for my shame
I shall sink into nothingness
Forgotten,—an eternal blame.
    Chicot's my name.

I am a jester. Would you know
Just what a jester claims to do?
I will enlighten you, and go
The long list of our duties through.
Remember, I am jesting, though,
So that the half will not be true,
As on my lips these duties glow.
    My name's Chicot.

Tales of all kinds my lips can frame,
Riddles I have for you to guess,
And as a fun-maker I claim

THE JESTERS

Proudly the highest place, no less.
I can an ardent fancy tame
With a tale of true love's distress,
Or I can kindle fancy's flame.
   Chicot's my name.

My own self I can from me throw,
Be troubadour, or clown, and you
What lies behind need never know
Nor to my jest need find the clue.
For when I choose and will it so,
True tales are false and false ones true,
At will I cause new minds to grow.
   My name's Chicot.

While here I hope with skilful game
To lighten yon fair maid's distress,
The boredom in her heart to tame,
Her mind in lightsome joy to dress.
Nor shall I fail and win your blame
For this my task, I know, unless
Dame Nature fails to fan the flame.
   Chicot's my name.

Let others advertise. I know
You will soon see what I can do

ACT SECOND

And if it pleases you or no.
Therefore, why should I weary you
E'er I begin with "I do so,
And so"—(*points to the other jesters*)
>like yon poor little crew?
Why, an I please you not, I'll go.
>My name's Chicot.

(MAUTPRÉ, SOLANGE, *and* OLIVER *show signs of evident pleasure at this effort of* CHICOT'S. BAROCO *and* VULCANO *whisper together*)

BAROCO

He grinds out epigram as though he were a mill.

VULCANO

Leave me your cause in hand. I'll take it up. Be still.
(*To* CHICOT) In your impromptu, sir, how much is memory
Of other's wit?

CHICOT

>Your shaft does not come home to me,
My memory is short, so short it irks me sore.
Why! I cannot recall where I've seen you before,
Whether 'twas in a rout of cowards and poltroons
In the war, or with chains on your wrists as galloons,
(*Laughter*) In the king's galleys.

VULCANO, *furiously*
> Dare but say those words again —

SOLANGE, *frightened*
Hold him back, Oliver.

VULCANO
> I'll split your tongue in twain
For speaking them.

CHICOT
> To us our speech is like his sword
To a brave belted knight. We jesters use a word
As the wasps use their sting, as the hawks use their beak,
And when we know its use to wound have but to speak.
You attacked, I replied. (*Turning his back on him and speaking to* DE MAUTPRÉ) Sir, I repeat my plea,
And entreat you to let Chicot your servant be,
Servant and histrion, mimic, musician, I
Care not if I must clown, practise astrology,
Read your eyes (*to* SOLANGE) or the stars, tell you of treasure trove
In the seas, or unfold old tales of mirth and love.
Mine is no purchased zeal. I would with humour gay

Brighten your eyes again, brighten this dungeon
  gray.
Lady, 'tis joy to serve when one so sweet commands,
Blows, even, were delight from such rose petal hands.
My heart lies on the ground longing to be your stool,
And 'tis an honest one, tho' the heart of a fool.
Swollen with pride, that heart no task could find
  more sweet
Than a footstool to be for your two tiny feet.

SOLANGE

No compliment was ever turned more prettily.

CHICOT

My heart instructs the lips; sweet lady, that is why.

VULCANO

The knave has wit.

NICOLE

    He speaks fine and soft, that young man,
His words fall on the ear like dripping in the pan.

CHICOT

So keenly felt, sweet maid, was my desire to-day
To be your slave, that crest and arms of de Maut-
  pré
I 'broidered on my coat.
(*He throws off his cloak and shows the* DE MAUTPRÉ

arms. At the same time everybody sees that he is humpbacked)

BAROCO

He is humpbacked! Oho!
An Aesop he may be, but not an Apollo.
(BAROCO *should almost crow the word* Apollo)

CHICOT

Of Aesop I have both the figure and the walk,
And like him, too, the pow'r to make a donkey talk.

OLIVER, *aside*

If he would wed Solange, this ornament is strange.
Why wear a thing which must a maiden's heart estrange?
He had no hump before.

SOLANGE

How sad that such a mind
As his in such a form by fate should be confined!

VULCANO

Three-cornered like his hat!

BAROCO

Like Pisa's tow'r he leans.

CHICOT

I see you wish to know, all of you, what this means.

ACT SECOND

SOLANGE

Nay, nay!

CHICOT

Oh, never fear to wound me. In a trice
You will see that to talk of it's no sacrifice.
You all think my hump a misfortune. Not a jot!
And I should pray to have a hump had I it not.
I'll add something which may perhaps astonish you,
Sometimes I feel regret that I cannot have two.
You glory in the straight backs God gave you, but know
If my back could be straight I would not have it so,
And though my hump may not find favour in your eyes,
Could I change it I would have one of twice the size.
Surely you know what luck a hump brings in its train
If you but touch it once. While if you touch again
Luck is yours all your life. Maidens of high degree
For just one single touch have sweetly smiled on me,
And lovers often beg upon my back to write
Their love-letters for luck. Merchants come in the night
And ask my hump to touch, and lest I fear the cold
Offer to warm the place with bags of good red gold.

Had I the taste to use my hump as use 't I can
I should not be here now; I 'd be a wealthy man.
Mines may be emptied, but never, it seems to me,
Can we quite exhaust all human credulity.
'T is enough nowadays an you 'd be rich or great
To have a crooked back—and—not to be quite straight.
Fools—amateurs—of me often delight to say
That from the casement my nurse let me drop one day.
No, sirs! When I was young I was as straight as you,
My back was flat and I was quite as foolish, too.
Then my brain grew and grew till my head was too small
To hold the brain which pressed hard on the frontal wall,
And all the doctors said that I was sure to die,
Killed by too great a brain—too much precocity.
One day my mother, as she bathed and dressed me, found
My forehead normal quite and on my back this mound
Of knowledge grown. My brain, ill at ease in my head,
Had found its way, while I lay fast asleep in bed,
Into snug quarters. Lest I pain should have endured

ACT SECOND

My mother kissed the place, and I, my friends, was cured.

VULCANO

This rogue must surely have the devil for a friend
If such case to his needs he can so neatly bend.
Answer him, Baroco. Cospetto! As I live,—
An answer some one must to him try to contrive,
Or he will win.

BAROCO

    Pray, what does the young man conclude
From this defence of his—er—I would not be rude—
Of his protuberance?

CHICOT

    Conclusions you require,
Baroco; your delightful crassness I admire.
I conclude that to have no hump upon your back
Shows that in common sense and in brain pow'r you lack,
And that your brainpan must rattle, it seems to me,
Your little brain about like a small dried-up pea.
(*General laughter*)

BAROCO

Why, you insult us all! Baron de Mautpré too!
He has no hump.

CHICOT

I know—But (*to* MAUTPRÉ), good my lord, with you

'Tis not the same. Your brain is stocked with all
   the lore
Of the long line of great men who have gone before.
There is no need for you to have as great a size
Of brain as I. You draw wisdom from Paradise.

MAUTPRÉ, *laughing*

Nay, now, Chicot. No more. For if I list to you
Longer I shall regret I am not hunchbacked too.

BAROCO, *to* CHICOT

Prithee one question more. Gifted one, tell us why
Such a rare bird as you from his gilt cage could fly,
Tell us why your last lord from his Chicot did part.

CHICOT

Ah, wretched man! You must, I see, revive the smart
Of vain regret, and with this question must enforce
Me to feel bitter pangs of never stilled remorse.
(*Very solemnly*) Why did I leave him? Why? To
   Heaven oft I've cried
Up the same question. Know, it was my fault he died.
Struck (*everybody shudders*) by a jest of mine
   which I had made too well,
My noble master laughed till his sides cracked, and
   fell
Into ten thousand bits! Yes, at my joke accurst,

ACT SECOND

My master laughed and died. For he laughed till he burst.

MAUTPRÉ

So! (*To* VULCANO) To all five now show the rooms where they may sleep,
And ev'ry day on the terrace above the keep
We will hold tourney, till after the thirty days
My daughter shall award her meed of blame or praise,
Shall choose the jester who shall remain in our pay
And with his wit amuse fair Solange de Mautpré.
(*Everybody rises*)

OLIVER
to VULCANO, *pointing to* HILARIUS, BAROCO, *and* JACK PUDDING

Let none of these approach the cellar door too near.

VULCANO

I have concealed the key.

OLIVER
Where?

VULCANO
In my pocket here.

(*All go out except* DE MAUTPRÉ *and his daughter, who go up to the window and remain there, talking, and* OLIVER, NARCISSUS, *and* CHICOT. *As the jesters go out,*)

HILARIUS

I hope my room is near the wine vaults, I am dry.

PUDDING

I hope the kitchen is not too far off.

OLIVER
who has been talking to CHICOT *and* NARCISSUS

       Now I
Will show you to your rooms. The Baron listens.
 (*Changing his voice and speaking sharply*) Now
You two have surely gazed down on those fields enow!
Come with me. Would you keep me waiting here
 all day?
Come with me, sirs. (*The* BARON *turns to the window
 again*)

      Excuse this rudeness, sirs, I pray.
(*They go out*)

MAUTPRÉ, *to* SOLANGE

Ah, may you, sweet, be cured by this odd remedy!

SOLANGE

It is a good one, father, for my malady.

MAUTPRÉ, *kisses her and going out*

Her forehead is quite cool, her colour unchanged.
 Still,
Oliver, who's a leech, says she is very ill. (*Exit*)

ACT SECOND

SOLANGE, *alone, meditatively*

How wondrously he speaks. All things he seems to know;
I wonder how he came to be a clown, Chicot!
Were he a noble—Oh, how lonely I have been.—
He's but a low-born clown— and I am seventeen.

(*She goes back to the window and does not see* OLIVER, NARCISSUS, *and* CHICOT *who come in quietly*)

CHICOT

She is there. Speak to her. Both of us long to learn
What she thought of us. Go.

NARCISSUS

With impatience I burn.
Pray ask her.

OLIVER

Well, Solange?

SOLANGE

Oliver?

NARCISSUS

to CHICOT, *continuing an argument begun outside*

It is true
Her eyes were turned to me tho' her ears turned to you.
She listened while you spoke, attention never slept,
But 't was always on me her lovely eyes were kept.

CHICOT

Why, man, she drank my words.

OLIVER

    And so my young men gain
Upon acquaintance, eh? Which for my lady's train
Would she prefer?

SOLANGE, *carelessly*

   I' faith, old friend, I hardly know.
Narcissus handsome is, brimful of wit Chicot.
Both are but servants, though. (*Dreaming again*)
 If Chicot count had been,
And I a lady-in-waiting upon the queen,
Narcissus a young lord—then—

OLIVER

    Then?

SOLANGE

    I do not know.
Oh, Oliver, my friend, why do you plague me so?
This tourney's meaning you to me have not explained,
My illness, and the clowns. By these what will be gained?
I'm lonely yet. Where is my fairy prince, I pray?
You promised one should come.

OLIVER, *embracing her affectionately*
>Child, he—is on the way.

CURTAIN

THE THIRD ACT

ACT THIRD

The terrace above the keep. A broad and beautiful terrace, with a magnificent view over the country. It is late afternoon of a glorious summer day. The sun sets during the course of the act. As the curtain rises JACQUES, JULIAN, *and* PIERRE, *dressed as men-at-arms, loll about and chat.*

JACQUES

How hot it is! This stone bench upon which I lie
Is like an oven's shelf, and I feel like a pie
Crusted with steel.

PIERRE

    Were I an enemy to scan
I'd give him my cuirass in exchange for a fan.

JULIAN

I would right gladly give him up the postern key
If he would find a place where I could cooler be.

PIERRE

I too would yield him up the castle in a trice
If in my mouth he'd drop a little piece of ice.

JACQUES

In this heat but few wake. 'T is hard that we should
 be

Posted here under arms to please the fantasy
Of Vulcano.

PIERRE
And this without a crown for pay!

JACQUES
I shall talk to Chicot about our wrongs to-day;
He with a quip can speak about this chest of gold
Which warmed our fancies, but which leaves our pockets cold.
But why does Vulcano keep us so long on guard?

PIERRE
I can smell dinner stewing.

JACQUES
So can I. 'T is hard.
A captain at this hour should not expect his troop
To conquer hunger's pangs, but to attack the soup.

JULIAN, *uncorking his flask and raising it*
When 't is so hot as this I sometimes wish that I
Had been born without hands and without arms.

Enter VULCANO

PIERRE
But why?

JULIAN
Why? Why, because I then no work need try to do.

ACT THIRD

I'd rest, and eat, and sleep, and drink a year or two.

(*He raises his bottle to his lips.* VULCANO, *who is behind him, takes it out of his lifted hand*)

VULCANO

Numskull and triple dolt! Did you then never think
That without hands you could not unassisted drink?
(JULIAN *makes a grab for his bottle, but* VULCANO *keeps it out of his reach*)
Oh! You will answer me, that dogs and cats, mayhap,
With head bent drink their fill. No, fool! They can but lap,
And lapping you do miss the savour of the wine
(*Drinks*) Which we enjoy who use of hand and lip combine.
Why! drinking is an art! First one delights the eye
With the red fire which gleams thro' the wine cheerily.
Then our nose humes its scent, and then our greedy lip,
Moist, eager with desire, takes one first tiny sip.
Master Tongue follows, tastes, passes the good wine to
Dame Palate, who enjoys the molten rubies, who,

Having enjoyed them, lets the red wine, drop by drop,
Roll slowly down our throat. Then for a while we stop,
Teasing our appetite until we can no more
Outrival Tantalus, and then we open door,
Let the wine gurgle down in its perfumèd stream
Until Silenus' self does not our rival seem.
So with unending care, and not as filthy swine
Slobber their hogwash down, varlets, should you drink wine,
And I am glad I seized bottle and chance before
You had the time to drink your wine wrong any more.
Go, now, and eat your fill and pray tell Baroco
That I would speak with him. Off with ye, varlets, go!

(*He throws* JULIAN *his empty bottle*)

JACQUES

Here the man comes.

(*Exeunt the men-at-arms. Enter* BAROCO, *who is finishing his dinner*)

VULCANO

What now! Red, and all out of breath?

ACT THIRD

BAROCO

Lord!

VULCANO

Your mouth full, chewing your dinner still! God's death!
This is no man of brain and wit whose ev'ry mood
Turns upon song, it is but a great sack of food.

BAROCO

My appetite is good.

VULCANO

But your position bad
Unless at once you set your brain to work, my lad.

BAROCO

Bad?

VULCANO

Aye! You greedy knave! See you not that Chicot
Crushes you all? That you all will most surely go
Out on the road again unless you prove that you
Can turn an epigram, something save eat can do?
Each ev'ning, as you know, fair Solange does propound
A subject upon which with touch light or profound
Each jester must devise. Each ev'ning you are left
By Chicot far behind. Art of all sense bereft
That you no effort make? He has a touch so sure

That ev'ry day he makes his chance the more secure.
Yester eve 'twas the moon, who was, he said, an old
Fairy transformed because of her great love of gold
Into a cheese by a mighty magician's spell,
And now lies shivering down in the castle well.
Then 'twas the glow-worms, which Chicot declared to be
The souls of children. But, Baroco, you must see
That unless you, too, can something of wit devise
You must, all surely, fail in this your enterprise.
To-day, again, will meet here Mautpré's court of wit,
Have you, then, aught prepared for when you're called to it?

(BAROCO *shakes his head*)

Nothing! And once again like a whipped cur you'll go
To your beds vanquished by that knave of knaves Chicot.
Your wit to his is like a burnt brand to the sun,
What he is finishing you, fool, have not begun,
And you must something find, for the month passes by
And a choice will be made, when 'tis a surety
Fair Solange will declare Narcissus or Chicot

ACT THIRD 103

The tourney's victor, and your day's done, Baroco.

BAROCO

Dio! And once again must I go hungry! I—

VULCANO

Not if you effort make. This ev'ning you must try
To better what Chicot devises.

BAROCO

So I will.

VULCANO

Then come! And search your brain for sentiments
 until
The tourney opens. Come with me and I will oil
Your rusty brain so that invention's arduous toil
Shall be more easy. I have a liqueur below
Which shall help you to find an answer to Chicot.
Courage then, and anon your eloquence shall be
An honour to myself, thyself, and Italy!

(*They go out. Enter* NARCISSUS *and* CHICOT)

NARCISSUS

At last the hour draws nigh when one can breathe
 again.

CHICOT, *looking at the sunset*

The hour, say rather, when a man must feel how
 vain

Is unbelief. The hour when God chose to impart
The first seeds of belief to ev'ry doubting heart.
Look at the sky. See how its robe of blue and white
Has purpled into crimson and to gold to-night,
Then watch the sunbeams die, God putting out the flame,
While the whole world in pray'r murmurs its Master's name.

NARCISSUS

You are quite lyric, friend! Have you turned poet too
As well as jester? What can have come over you?

CHICOT

Nay, Robert, mock me not. There comes to ev'ry one
A day when, wondering, watching the setting sun,
Mystery fills the soul, the heart swells and the eyes
Fill with tears, yearning for a distant Paradise.
We feel more deeply all that happens and we move
Along life's path in dreamland, for we are in love.

NARCISSUS

In love? Then fair Solange, my friend, has conquered you,
The man of wit.

CHICOT

Mock not. Mock not.

ACT THIRD

NARCISSUS
after a slight pause and quite simply and quietly
         I love her too.

CHICOT
So shall our bet lead on to word warfare and strife—

NARCISSUS
In which the one must win, the other lose, a wife.

CHICOT
Do you your best, my friend! I for my part shall do
All a man can to win Solange's hand from you.

NARCISSUS
And I from you that hand to win shall try. I fear
You, René, more to-night, though, than—

CHICOT
        Hush! They are here.

(*Enter from the castle* SOLANGE, MAUTPRÉ, OLIVER, NICOLE, JACQUES, PIERRE, *and* JULIAN, *and a little later* VULCANO *and* BAROCO. *From the other side enter* JACK PUDDING *and* HILARIUS)

OLIVER
Come, sound the bugle call. The tourney must begin!

All take your places.—You, Pierre, call our people
  in.
(*All take their places*)

SOLANGE

I love the breeze of evening now that the sun
Has sunk to rest. To-day true pleasure was there
  none
In active movement. I slumbered thro' half the day
Watching from under heavy lids my dog at play,
Too hot to play myself, too hot to feed my dove,
Too hot for needlework, too hot indeed to move.

NARCISSUS

Had I, fair lady, an enchanter's magic pow'r
You had not suffered from the heat a single hour.

SOLANGE

What had you done?

NARCISSUS

    I had become a storm to quell
The sun's hot rays with rain.

CHICOT

      And I my magic spell
I would, had I possessed the power, used to blow
The sun out altogether.

ACT THIRD

SOLANGE

               No, indeed, Chicot,
That would have frightened me.

CHICOT

               Then, lady, would I bend
The swallows to my wish, and ev'ry bird should lend
Their flapping wings to fan with gently soothing stir
The breezes round your head and neck.

SOLANGE

                     I thank you, sir,
Now I am better.

OLIVER

           Come. The tourney we begin,
Which, of our jesters here, but one alone can win.
Your places, pray. Here sits the queen and here the king,
The others here and here will form the jousting ring
In which with ready wit you five brave fools shall fight.
Knights of the cap and bells, prepare! Be sure the right
God will defend.

VULCANO

'Tis well. Art ready, Baroco?

BAROCO

who is slightly excited by the wine he has drunk and who has the bottle with him

Ready am I and primed brimful, my Vulcano!
This wine is Moses' staff which can set free the stream
Of wit from stony brains, and I have dreamed a dream!
You shall see, Vulcano, me carry off the prize
And win distinction in our gentle lady's eyes.

VULCANO, *uneasily*

Have you not drunk too much?

OLIVER

      Now an our lady please
To name a subject for discourse?

SOLANGE

      I name the breeze
Of which we have just spoken. 'Tis to-night my whim
That each do tell us what the breeze suggests to him.

OLIVER, *announcing*

The breeze!

ACT THIRD

CHICOT

A pretty subject.

HILARIUS

A sad one.

BAROCO

Confused.

OLIVER

Hilarius, you first. Now, sir, keep us amused.

HILARIUS

The breeze. (*A pause*)

MAUTPRÉ

Well, sir?

HILARIUS

The breeze howls through the winter night,
Keeps us awake and drives the women mad with fright,
Lugubriously howls and whistles on its way.
Death on its path it spreads, horror and wild dismay,
Death on the ships at sea, widows along the shore,
Misery, wounds, and death.

MAUTPRÉ

We prithee, sir, no more!

This wit of yours is grim and makes our blood run
  cold.

    HILARIUS, *more dolefully than ever*
I am gay as a rule and I am always told
That my wit lightsome is and as a song-bird gay.
You must excuse me if family cares to-day
Sadden me.

    OLIVER
        Far from me be it your grief to blame,
But I would fain point out that each day 't is the
  same.
Every day your tale is a dark tale of woe.
We asked for jesters.

    HILARIUS
        Well? Am I no jester?

    OLIVER
                    No.
If my opinion should weigh with you in the least
I would suggest that you become a Trappist priest.
'T is your vocation.

    MAUTPRÉ
        Now, Narcissus, an it please
You to stand forth, we'd hear you discourse on the
  breeze.

ACT THIRD

NARCISSUS

There's elegance in the breeze.
She is so debonair,
Softens the summer heat,
Ripples a maiden's hair
With a desire to please.
There's elegance in the breeze.

There's cleverness in the breeze.
Without her aid each fold
Of this my cloak would hang
Heavily, stiffly cold,
Cold as life's ironies.
There's cleverness in the breeze.

The breeze is a winsome maid,
Merrily, gaily bright,
Frolicsome, with a depth
Of human love to-night,
Warmhearted, unafraid.
The breeze is a winsome maid.

The breeze is fantastic, she
Loves with light things to play,
Lifting up, sweeping off
All that endure her sway,

In a whirlwind of glee.
The breeze has her fantasy.

The breeze is the soldier's friend,
Spreads with her forceful wave
The flapping flag which makes
Even a coward brave
To attack or defend.
The breeze is the soldier's friend.

The breeze is the friend of love,
Whirling my heart to meet
Happiness, untold joy,
Low at my lady's feet,
Then up, her eyes to greet,
And its devotion prove.
The breeze is the friend of love.

Lady, I love the breeze,
For she is ne'er the same,
Understands ev'ry move
In life's bewild'ring game.
May she aid me to please!
Lady, I love the breeze.

MAUTPRÉ

'T is marvellous well turned, Narcissus. Is't not so, Solange?

ACT THIRD

SOLANGE

Indeed 'tis clever.

VULCANO, *aside*
                What says Baroco?

BAROCO

It is well turned, quite well; indeed, 'tis wondrous fine,
But do but wait, my friend, until you have heard mine.

SOLANGE

Narcissus until now is champion of the breeze.
Who takes the gauntlet up, our minds and ears to please?

OLIVER

Jack Pudding's next. Nicole! Your seat I prithee keep.

NICOLE
who has risen and is gazing in open-mouthed admiration at NARCISSUS

His beauty would a maiden's virtue send to sleep.
Beshrew me! He is handsome.

MAUTPRÉ
              Now, Jack Pudding, pray,
Your discourse on the breeze are we to hear to-day?

JACK PUDDING, *with a silly chuckle*

I dunno if the breeze is the friend of a clown,
But I know that to home it blows ripe apples down.
(*Everybody laughs,* JACK PUDDING *more loudly than the rest*)

VULCANO

Furbish your wit up; try, now, my friend Baroco,
These gentlefolk of France your poet's gift to show,
Give them now of your best and you must surely win.

BAROCO

My trouble is that I scarce know where to begin,
So much have I to say. Is it my turn now?

OLIVER

No!
(*There is a movement of general interest and attention*)
Upon the breeze the next to discourse is Chicot.

CHICOT

The gentle breeze which stirs the leaves of yonder vine
Recalls to me a tale—a favourite of mine,
A story which one day in an old book I found,
An ancient tome, gaunt, grim, black-lettered, leather-bound,

ACT THIRD 115

Which tome, looking as though 'twere filled with tales of sin,
Promised but little of the charm I found within.
'Twas in this book I read the tale which, if you please,
I will repeat to-night—The Story of the Breeze.
A breeze one day, abroad on fun or mischief bent,
Entered a castle grim, traversed the battlement,
And on the terrace found, sitting and spinning there,
A maiden of sixteen, blue-eyed, with golden hair.
Blue were her eyes, and soft as the young sky at dawn,
Or the waves of the lake the breeze had crossed that morn,
And as th' intruder loosed a strand of golden hair
The maid looked up and laughed, so sweet, so chaste, so fair,
That the breeze, who till then had kissed and whirred away
Over the trees and far, fickle until to-day,
Knew that this time his heart was bound and tethered there
To that child of sixteen, blue-eyed, with golden hair,
For the fair maid had won, won all unconsciously,
A lover without name and whom she could not see,

While the breeze loved to love, and for no royal throne
Would have exchanged his right to love her thus unknown.
Then, as he could not bring her flowers all abloom,
The butterflies he'd waft in shoals into her room
From forest glades and fields, from near and far, and they,
Blue, yellow, red, and green, a quivering bouquet,
He blew into her hair, bejewelled it, and then,
When he grew jealous, swiftly blew them out again.
The scent of new-mown hay he brought in from the fields,
From ev'ry bush and flow'r what each of sweetest yields,
Marjoram, meadow-sweet, and sage he carried there,
For the maid of sixteen, blue-eyed, with golden hair.
Sometimes he'd wander off, down into far Provence,
And from the fairest lands of the fair land of France
He would come laden back with orange blossoms' breath,
Which he had stolen e'er men crushed the blooms to death.
For all that ailed the maid he found a ready cure;
Were the day stormy, he would fetch her air more pure

ACT THIRD

From snowy mountain-tops, and if she were cold, why,
His own love blew so warm he warmed her easily.
When she was reading in works of old bard or sage,
The breeze was waiting there to help her turn the page.
And when at night she slept in her white-curtained bed,
He'd venture till he touched his darling's golden head,
And, drunken with the joy forbidden, dare to sip
A kiss that maddened him from the child's smiling lip.
One day, alas! there came a lord from Aquitaine
To woo and win the maid. He came and came again,
And the unhappy breeze howled in his mad despair.
Gone the maid of sixteen, blue-eyed, with golden hair,
Handsome the swain and rich, strong in his manhood's spring,
Blushes, a whispered word, the chaplain, and a ring.
What, when a wooer's young, rich, and has all to please,
What, against such a man, can the most perfumed breeze?

Off went the breeze, and rushed heartbroken, desire-torn,
Into the desert, where, anguished, alone, forlorn,
He gathered strength to rush back with unwonted might,
Batter the castle walls, howl, the unhappy wight,
As though his storm-tossed soul could in the noise find peace,
Or, with a whirl of rage, could his poor heart release,
And when the sexton old rang out the marriage bell
So fiercely blew that he tolled a funereal knell.
So that no flow'rs should deck the couple's bridal way,
Every rose-bush he swept into sad disarray,
Murdering all the blooms he had caressed of old,
For the sixteen-year bride, blue-eyed, with hair of gold.

NICOLE

He's set me weeping.

JACQUES

    I tremble the end to know.

SOLANGE

Poor little breeze!

ACT THIRD

MAUTPRÉ

Upon your lips we hang, Chicot,
Finish your story. We are anxious all, my friend,
With what you've said entranced, to hear how it will end.

CHICOT

Off and away the breeze, sweeping a weary world,
Off and away he went, misery tossed and whirled,
Came back in two years' time, back to the castle old,
Where dwelt the sweet young wife, blue-eyed, with hair of gold;
Back to the castle grim, and in a cradle there
Found a wee baby girl, blue-eyed, with golden hair.
Gently and softly blew, turning the child's toy mill,
Eager to win a smile where he had come to kill;
Turning the tiny mill as he had kissed of old
The mother's sweet blue eyes and hair of burnished gold,
Then sank to endless rest under the mother's chair,
To dream of her blue eyes and of her golden hair.
(All applaud)

SOLANGE

I cannot speak my thanks.

MAUTPRÉ

    A charming legend.

VULCANO, *to* BAROCO

                    You
Must now tell yours.

SOLANGE

    With pleasure I my duty do,
And for to-day with wreath of laurel crown Chicot
The victor of the breeze's tourney.

VULCANO

                  Lady, no!
E'er you decide you must my friend Baroco hear.

MAUTPRÉ

We'll hear him. Justice is to all our hearts most
    dear.
Now, sirrah!

VULCANO

    Now, my friend! Repeat the legend fine
You promised me, and show yourself a Florentine.

BAROCO

Er—he—

VULCANO

    Per Bacco! Now what has come over you?
Speak up, man!

ACT THIRD

CHICOT

That I fear is more than he can do.

VULCANO

Silence, I beg.

BAROCO

He—Haw— (*All laugh*)

VULCANO

My friend shall speak, I say.

CHICOT

By all means, if he can. But he does naught but bray!

BAROCO, *with much difficulty*

Not on me, sirs and dames, is't fair to lay the blame,
I had a legend, but—but Chicot's was the same.

(*General laughter.* VULCANO *shakes* BAROCO *rudely*)

VULCANO

Drunkard!

BAROCO, *very drunk*

Your wine was very potent. Do not touch
Me, sir! How could I dream that I had drunk too much?
'T was sweet as milk. (*Lurching over to* CHICOT)
He stole—

CHICOT

Holà! Hold up there! Well,
Baroco wishes me the tale for him to tell
Which he upon the breeze had ready, and which now
Emotion deep has stilled in his full throat, I trow.
An hour agone our friend, the noble Baroco,
Feeling athirst had drunk his usual draught,—you know
He drinks but water,—and he lay and took his ease
Upon the terrace, when the wicked summer breeze
Quaffed from his purpled face its winey colour, then
Between his open lips swift blew it in again.
When with some effort he to his feet did arise
Baroco found that he, to his intense surprise,
Could neither walk nor run. His face was not as red
As it had been, but he, poor man, was drunk instead.
The breeze which ev'ry day passes him, I suppose,
Had made him drunk with wine quaffed from his purple nose.

BAROCO

(*lurches forward to attack* CHICOT *and nearly falls.* VULCANO *holds him up*)
Did you hear what he said? I must—

VULCANO

What can you do,

ACT THIRD

You drunken pig? If I did not look after you,
Why, what would happen?

BAROCO
     I should fall down, I suppose.
But look at me and say, have I a purple nose?
I'm nearly sober. Why should crook-backed Chicot scoff?
He can't walk straight, can he, nor sleep his hump-back off
Like I my drink?

VULCANO
  Come, now!
   (*Exeunt* VULCANO *and* BAROCO)

JULIAN, *to* JACQUES
     Speak to him now.

JACQUES, *mysteriously*
       Chicot,
We want to ask you, for so wondrous well you know
How to put words in place as they should be, to plead
Our cause, for you alone can help us in our need.

CHICOT
Your need?

JACQUES
Our purse's need.

PIERRE
The treasure must be found.

JULIAN
We must be paid. What good is gold when under ground?

CHICOT
Have all of you gone mad? What is it you would ask?

JACQUES
Hunting for buried treasure is a thankless task
Unless where it is buried one may know, and then —

PIERRE
It needs no sage to go and dig it up again.

CHICOT
What buried treasure?

JACQUES
Why, that of our wages, man.

CHICOT
Beshrew me if your mystery now probe I can.

JACQUES
Come with us. We'll explain.

(JACQUES, PIERRE, *and* JULIAN *go out with* CHICOT)

ACT THIRD

MAUTPRÉ

who has been talking to OLIVER *and* SOLANGE, *to* SOLANGE

Your eyes are overbright,
Your cheek is flushed, your chamber waits for you.
Good-night.

(MAUTPRÉ *goes out.* OLIVER *and* SOLANGE *remain, talking together.* NICOLE, *who has been hovering around* NARCISSUS, *approaches him*)

NICOLE, *slyly*

Narcissus.

NARCISSUS

Dame Nicole?

NICOLE, *timidly*

Nay, 't were no burning shame
If you should say Nicole to me, without the "dame."

NARCISSUS, *smiling*

Nicole, then.

NICOLE, *offers him a rose*

See, it is the colour of your hose
And of your doublet. So accept from me this rose.

NARCISSUS, *taking the rose, but looking puzzled*

Thank you, Nicole.

NICOLE, *growing more and more enthusiastic*
>> Let it my feeling for me speak,
For it is red as is with shame each burning cheek
Of poor Nicole. (NARCISSUS *draws away from her*)
>> Nay, nay. Draw not thus off afar,
Draw nearer rather. (*With a sudden outburst*)
>> What a handsome man you are!
And what an air! Alas! I am a weakling—

NARCISSUS, *trying to stop her*
>> Dame—

NICOLE

Hush! I have ne'er endured such burning, such sweet shame
As now. But when below, down in the kitchen there,
A burnished platter tells me that my face is fair,
I think of you, my lord Narcissus, and I can
Swear that no heart could beat for a more proper man.

NARCISSUS

But I—

NICOLE
>> I have for years some little store put by
Of crowns, and we could live, Narcissus, wondrously
Snug.

NARCISSUS
>> We? Then you suggest—?

ACT THIRD

NICOLE
    That we two should be wed,
That you should (*taking his hand*) share with me
 my fortune and (*coyly*) my bed.

NARCISSUS
Nicole, you flatter me. But I have taken vow
Never to wed. It is too late to tell you now
The why and wherefore, but, alas, it cannot be.
Good night, Nicole, good night, and do not dream
 of me.
Take with you to your couch, to read, your kitchen
 book.   (*As he goes off*)
Solange I would have won and I have—pleased
 the cook.
(*He goes out laughing*)

NICOLE
He's young and timid yet—a woman's craft and
 will
Over his bashfulness may be triumphant still.
(*She goes after him*)

OLIVER
Solange, child, have you thought that the time now
 draws near
To choose your jester? What of Narcissus?

SOLANGE

                               I fear
That he would cloy my taste. He thinks but of his hose,
His doublet, and himself. Speak to him, into pose
Instinctively he falls, for admiration cries,
And looks himself o'er with ever adoring eyes.
He is too elegant by far. What need, I ask,
If the wine have fine flavour, for so fine a flask?
Why need the outer man be dressed in clothes so grand
When, were they there, we could his virtues understand
Under a humbler garb. Narcissus' flask is fine,
But, Oliver, I do not think I like the wine.

OLIVER, *aside*

Dear crystal heart! (*Aloud*) Then which, child, of the other four
Who have assembled, than Narcissus pleases more
My sweet Solange?

SOLANGE

               Why, not that drunkard Baroco,
Hilarius, or Jack. There is but one,— Chicot.
And were he not crook-backed, oh, Oliver, he'd be—

ACT THIRD

OLIVER

Yes, dear, he would be what?

SOLANGE, *with a little sigh*
                Perfect, it seems to me.

OLIVER, *aside*
I think I understand.

SOLANGE
                Ah, friend! Did you but know
What wondrous flow'rs of thought from the mind of Chicot
Sprout for my pleasure! He looks first into mine eyes,
Then pours his fancies out, witty or wondrous wise,
Just as my fancy bids. Weaves me a legend, and
The whole world lies within the hollow of my hand.
He, first of all men, has successfully brought light
Into the darkness of my ignorance's night,
He has with words my prison walls pierced thro' and thro',
Has opened out beyond a fair horizon, too,
And, Oliver, he has such seeds of knowledge sown
That he has made my very mind and heart his own.
When he is gay I laugh, when sad, I am distressed,
And of the two I hardly know which is the best.

OLIVER, *slyly*

He makes you weep? Why, then, Solange, it seems to me
He is no jester.

SOLANGE, *to herself*
Ah! If he could only be
Of noble birth and if his back were only straight.

OLIVER

These things occur sometimes, Solange, to those who wait
Their time—

SOLANGE
What mean you?

OLIVER
Naught. But I have heard it said
That crookbacks lose their humps the night before they wed.
It is but idle superstition, of course.

SOLANGE
Oh!
Then he must wed to lose it, must he? Poor Chicot!

(OLIVER *makes a sign to* CHICOT, *who is visible in the wing, and goes out leaving* CHICOT *and* SOLANGE *together*)

ACT THIRD

CHICOT

Sighing, my lady? Sad? Why, such things cannot be,
Sadness must always be the child of memory,
And memory for you, Lady Solange, can ne'er
Hold aught but gladness and joy. Surely one so fair,
On life's fair journey now but starting, cannot yet
Have ground for sighs, which are the voices of regret.

SOLANGE

Who knows what grief the fates may have for me in store?
I tremble as a ship which, pushed off from the shore,
Quivers and faces the horizon, knowing naught
Of dangers with which ev'ry voyage must be fraught.

CHICOT

Danger from off your path, sweet maid, will disappear,
Horizon brighten, when your dainty bark draws near,
And my prophetic eye beyond it clearly sees
A vista of an isle set with groves of great trees,
Under whose shade all fears of unknown danger cease,
And you live radiant in one sweet eternal peace.

Run down your little ship, fair lady, from the shore,
Launch it, and let your fears be stilled for evermore.
For you, sweet maid, a life I can and do assure
Of happiness and peace, in safety and secure.
(*With growing tenderness*)
An alchemist who sought perfection's purity
Would have, Solange, to seek what God has given thee,
For thou hast ev'ry gift. A name so sweet to voice
That it, as thou art, was, I can but think, God's choice.
A mouth so gently pure and lips so free from guile
That from them I believe the angels learned to smile.
Blue eyes so deep, so good, so earnest, I can tell
Their secret. They have been and are Truth's holy well,
And the deep azure which their bright depths glows within
Was garnered from the skies when they were Seraphin.
Your eyes in grandeur born have remained large, and show
Wide-opened wonder at the smallness here below,
And with the glory of their wondrous heav'nly birth
They put to shame all that is impure here on earth.

ACT THIRD

SOLANGE

Chicot, what are you saying?

CHICOT

Sweet Solange, your soul
To open to the sunlight is my life's one goal,
So that in after years you shall remember how
One summer's eve we sat where we are sitting now,
And how a fool who had learned wisdom sitting there
Was the first man to tell you, sweet, that you are fair.
Ah, child! Such words as these you oft again will hear
From other lips than mine. But in your shell-like ear
I first have whispered them; trembling I first have drawn
Upon that lovely cheek womanhood's early dawn
Incarnate in a sweetly hot encarmined blush,
Painted on velvet tissue with impassioned brush,
Another's voice to you the selfsame words may say,
But first from me, Solange, you have heard them to-day,
And when that other comes he cannot take from me
The treasure of to-night stored in my memory.

SOLANGE

Another who shall come? I do not understand
Who he may be.

CHICOT

    He is crowned king in that fair land
I have described. He will your heart most surely move
And fill to overflow. His name, Solange, is Love.

SOLANGE

Love? What is love?

CHICOT

    Alas! poets have tried alway
What King Love is and does with woven words to say.
To paint his godlike virtues and his vices, all
Their minds and all their weft of words have proved too small.
Love is a gift from Hell, an evil from above,
A deadly poison which one loves to take is Love,
A poison which imbibed causes terrific pain,
For which all mortals who have tasted strive again.
Love is, will always be, life in a little space,
For death lurks in a "no," life wells up in a "yes."
Love is the mighty force which leads to Paradise
Over the foul morass of human prejudice.

ACT THIRD

To love is on your road a second self to find
Whose soul with yours shall be forever fast entwined,
For they were born as twins beneath God's golden throne,
And so born He will not let either live alone.
Love so met is the friend to whom your heart goes straight,
For whom your heart, throughout, has always seemed to wait,
Who is yours and you his, in whose voice is the ring
To which your heart rings back in spite of ev'rything.
Love speaks. What matter, then, fortune or rank to you?
Love is the master. Do you understand?

        SOLANGE, *in a low voice*

                              I do.

(SOLANGE *and* CHICOT *rise from the seat on which they were sitting.* SOLANGE *drops, as if by accident, a rose, which* CHICOT *picks up and presses to his lips. As* SOLANGE *goes slowly out,* CHICOT *stands gazing after her*)

        VERY SLOW CURTAIN

THE FOURTH ACT

ACT FOURTH

The castle keep, overgrown with creepers, flowers, moss, and ivy, with the old postern gate, through which access may be gained into the castle. A pathway runs around the top of the keep wall, up to which the characters can climb by a small stone stair. BAROCO, HILARIUS, *and* JACK PUDDING *are discovered as the curtain rises. They are preparing their bundles for departure.*

JACK PUDDING

WELL, we must go, it seems.

BAROCO

No more de Mautpré's wine
Will, trickling down, console this thirsty throat of mine.

HILARIUS

No more de Mautpré's fowls, their breasts so plump, so white,
Boiled or roast, shall I have to stay my appetite.

BAROCO

The devil take Narcissus and crook-backed Chicot!
The month is over and we three must surely go,
For when Solange this evening shall choose, not you
Nor I shall win, but one out of those cursèd two.

HILARIUS

Yes, we shall surely leave the castle of Mautpré
To-morrow at the latest. I am far from gay
When I think of the future.

BAROCO

                      Say you so? And I
Could, when I think of it, with raging fury cry
Out on my belly, for I know not where nor how
I shall find meat nor drink with which to fill it now.

JACK PUDDING

Well, since Mautpré will not accept my jest nor song,
I'll take some apples in my pack with me. (*He goes out*)

HILARIUS

                              I long
So for those tender birds that, lest my heart should break,
I'll go and wring a neck or two for friendship's sake,
And take them with me. (*He goes out*)

BAROCO

                I some wine will pack away
Snug in this bottle, for I fear I shall not stay
After to-night.

ACT FOURTH

Enter VULCANO

VULCANO

Holà! What have you tied up there
Into that bundle?

BAROCO

Sir, the few poor rags I wear,
And these (*holds bundle up*) are all the goods that
  I, poor fool, possess.
I leave the castle, sir, in truly deep distress.

VULCANO

You leave it? You intend to leave us, Baroco?

BAROCO

Since no one can prevent my going, sir, I go.

VULCANO

Nobody can prevent? How mean you? Cannot I —

BAROCO

Nay, my lord, you shall not through me court in-
  jury.
These jesters twain, of whom Solange one will ap-
  point
To-night to stay, have put our noses out of joint.

VULCANO

Our noses?

BAROCO

      Aye, indeed! I shall not be perplexed
To guess whom they will try, sir, to get rid of next.

VULCANO

Can you mean me? (BAROCO *nods*) Get rid of *me?*
of Vulcano?

BAROCO

Why not, sir? They are strong in favour. You will go,
I trust, without a turmoil, will not, I suppose,
Be rash, resist them, and resort to threats or blows?

VULCANO, *furiously angry*

I will not? Aha! You, my friend, to-night shall see,
Whether I, Vulcano, can with impunity
Be bearded by this stripling pair.

BAROCO, *aside*

                  I'll not assuage
His anger once roused. He may help me in his rage.
(*Aloud*) Nay, sir, be patient. With affront and insult bear
As we have done, and go; for each must take his share
Of shame and cry content.

ACT FOURTH

VULCANO

Not I, by Mars! Ah, no!
They shall see what it means to insult Vulcano!
By Satan's cloven hoof, and by the two ram's horns
Upon his head! no man shall trample on my corns!
Upon my head I swear, by all that I hold dear
I now make oath, you shall alone be jester here!
Dost hear me, Baroco? Aye, if I have to pound
These walls into a powder, raze them to the ground,
Thou shalt be chosen and thou hast my plighted word.
Go put away that (*pointing to bundle*); I will fetch
and gird my sword. (*He goes out*)

BAROCO, *slyly*

Baroco is no fool. Methinks I've found the way
Into the graces of the Baron de Mautpré.

(*He goes out*)

Enter CHICOT, *followed by* JACQUES, JULIAN, *and* PIERRE

CHICOT

Be patient. You will see the Baron de Mautpré
Will pay you all in full.

JACQUES

But when?

PIERRE

"Some other day"
Of course. So 't was before and so 't will be again.
My patience has become too weak to bear the strain.

JULIAN

Always "to-morrow" 't is and always "patience" too.

Enter OLIVER

OLIVER

Grumbling again! I' faith, methinks a night or two
Down in the dungeon there would do ye grumblers good,
And make ye grumble at a far less wholesome food
Than Nicole serves ye. Or a thwacking blow or twain
From Vulcano's great staff might make for peace again.
In with ye all!

JACQUES

This time we'll say no more. Who knows
(*Sullenly*) Next time it may be we who can deal out the blows.

(*Exeunt* JACQUES, PIERRE, *and* JULIAN)

CHICOT, *to* OLIVER

Are we alone?

ACT FOURTH

OLIVER

We are.

CHICOT

Speak quickly. You have been
Down to the wood and you my man down there
have seen?

OLIVER

Yes.

CHICOT

Well? What did he say? Beshrew me! But a week
Passes between each two words you vouchsafe to
speak.

OLIVER

He told me that he had in readiness a horse,
Four men, and the great chest.

CHICOT

Yes, then?

OLIVER

I said, of course,
Just as you told me, that when he should see a white
Kerchief wave from above the battlemented height
Of Mautpré's castle, he should hasten here with
speed
With men, horse, and the chest.

CHICOT

       You are in very deed
A trusty friend to me, and I will tell you now
How I intend to slip past Mautpré's taken vow
Which ev'ry stranger knight from out this castle rude,
Lest he should see its poverty, would aye exclude.
De Mautpré's poor, I'm rich—

OLIVER

       You know him not, my friend.
It will be useless, quite, to offer him to lend
One crown, for de Mautpré is poor but proud. Your gold
He would refuse.

CHICOT

      I know. Let me my plan unfold.
Some days since, pressed for gold, de Mautpré told a tale
To Julian, Pierre, and Jacques, of treasure in some vale
Of his, deep buried by an ancestor, and he
Added that this great chest would soon discovered be.
Now I am rich and I this treasure chest have found.

ACT FOURTH

OLIVER

Found it?

CHICOT, *laughing*

Yes, and have found it on de Mautpré's ground.

OLIVER

I do not understand.

CHICOT

I spoke but half in fun
And half in sober earnest. Hark what I have done!
De Mautpré has within this castle gaunt and grim
A priceless treasure which is half unknown to him.

OLIVER

Unknown? A treasure? Here?

CHICOT

Solange's heart, I mean.

OLIVER

I see. You mean Solange—

CHICOT, *warmly*

Should be a crownèd queen
Were I but king. I love her, Oliver, far more
Than aught of all those things by which men set such store,
As much as honour, more, far more, than fame or wealth.

OLIVER

And so?

CHICOT

Her father I mean to enrich by stealth.

OLIVER

By stealth?

CHICOT

The man with whom you spoke my servant is,
And brings with him a key of gold.

OLIVER

These mysteries
Do irk my patience. What, now, is this key of gold?
Speak plainly, not in riddles, for I am too old
To grasp their meaning. You perchance in plainer speech
Can put the matter? Then do so, I do beseech.

CHICOT

I will. The chest which my man Hubert hither brings
Contains treasure of gold with jewels and with rings
Out of my store. The tale Baron de Mautpré told
I have made true. He has but to enjoy the gold.

OLIVER

If he refuse?

ACT FOURTH

CHICOT

That he will not, for I have taught
His lesson to each man of those who now have brought
The treasure, and each man his tale alike will tell
And like de Mautpré's own. Why, man, you know full well
That when the brass-bound chest of gold he doth perceive,
De Mautpré then and there his own tale will believe.
Then being rich again, thanks to this treasure trove,
My hope is he may smile on my tale of true love.
Now, friend, will you help me to win Solange for wife,
And by so doing make me your true friend for life?

OLIVER, *after a slight pause*

Aye, that I will, René, for I believe you love
Our little maid.

CHICOT

I swear by God who throned above
In Heaven hears me, Oliver, I swear I do.

OLIVER

Then may she find, I pray, de Chancenac, in you

A worthy husband. You may put your trust in me.
Tell me now what in this deceit my part shall be.

CHICOT

Little and much. Your part shall be from yonder tow'r
The handkerchief to wave at the appointed hour.
But hush! Somebody comes.

(*Enter at intervals* MAUTPRÉ *with* SOLANGE, NARCISSUS, VULCANO, *and* BAROCO, JACK PUDDING, HILARIUS, NICOLE, JACQUES, PIERRE, *and* JULIAN)

VULCANO

I tell you, Baroco,
That you shall stay.

JACQUES

I wonder why I tremble so.
I think, i'faith, tho' armed all three, we are afraid,
Tho' our opponents be two old men and a maid.

NICOLE, *looking at* NARCISSUS
Were mine the choice, I know —

OLIVER

Now take your places, pray!

ACT FOURTH

Our tourney's queen will choose the jester of Mautpré.

(*All arrange themselves as in* ACT THIRD)

MAUTPRÉ

Untrammelled, free as air, my child, select the fool
Whom you have chosen. For under your mimic
 rule
Each one has done his best. Speak.

SOLANGE

                        Him I choose is one
Whose weft of pleasantry and fund of harmless fun
Have charmed me.

JACK PUDDING
    'Tis my portrait, surely.

SOLANGE
                        He can be
At will witty or sad.

HILARIUS
    Sad? Why, she must mean me.

SOLANGE

Whiche'er he be he charms, with wit's unceasing
 flow
Or touching metaphor, our minds.

VULCANO
>'T is Baroco!

What other of them all with his gifts, I say, can
Have won such praise as this?

SOLANGE, *smiling*
>Nay, Chicot is the man.

VULCANO

Chicot! Nay, fair Solange, awry I surely hear,
Or you have failed to make, perhaps, your meaning clear.
Crook-backed Chicot! (*Laughs scornfully*)

NARCISSUS, *to* CHICOT
>You've won the bet.

CHICOT, *to* NARCISSUS
>And happiness.

BAROCO

I am undone.

VULCANO

>Come, come! What means this foolishness?

Do you, I ask, so far all clear perception lack
As to have chosen that mountainous crookèd back
To be your jester? Nay. You cannot mean it. Oh,
I understand. You would but jest with Vulcano.

ACT FOURTH

To see what I would say and do, you wished, and I
Almost fell in the trap you laid so cunningly.

MAUTPRÉ

Chicot is chosen by the queen. The tourney's o'er.

VULCANO, *furiously*

Chicot! Now let me not hear that name any more!
(*To* HILARIUS, JACK PUDDING, *and* NARCISSUS)
Be off, you three, at once. And you, sir, too must
  go. (*To* CHICOT)

BAROCO

And I?

VULCANO

The jester who shall stay is Baroco.

MAUTPRÉ

Am I not master here?

SOLANGE

Father!

CHICOT, *to* OLIVER

Run! Fetch us swords,
I'll make that braggart eat his vainly boasting
  words,
I have no doubt that he is quite used to the food,
And for each tear Solange has shed, a drop of blood
Shall Vulcano disgorge—

MAUTPRÉ, *to* SOLANGE
>Fear not, my child!

JACQUES, *to* PIERRE *and* JULIAN
>To act
Now is the time.

MAUTPRÉ, *to the jesters*
>Are all your goods and chattels packed?
(*Firmly*) Give each a small gift, Oliver, and let them go,
Hilarius, Jack Pudding, and you Baroco.
Farewell, Chicot is chosen jester of Mautpré.

VULCANO
Not Baroco?

MAUTPRÉ
>Enough. Go, sirrah!

VULCANO, *to* BAROCO
>You shall stay.
My word is plighted.

MAUTPRÉ
>What care I for your pledged word,
Are you the master? Ho there, some one, quick, my sword!

SOLANGE
Father, I beg—

ACT FOURTH

VULCANO

Do not I pray, fair lady, balk
Your father in his wish. 'T is time our swords should talk.

CHICOT

to OLIVER, *who has brought rapiers to him and to* NARCISSUS

Thank you, my friend. And now —

OLIVER

Nay, wait a moment's space,
The time is not yet ripe.

VULCANO

Once more, the jester's place
Is Baroco's. (*To the servants*) And will you, with me, not essay
From Mautpré's close-drawn purse now to extract the pay
Earned by your labour? 'T is time pride with beggared purse
Stepped down from horseback. Ye are certainly no worse
Than those who call themselves your masters, but refuse
To pay ye for your work with aught except abuse.

JACQUES

He's right.

PIERRE

Aye, he speaks sooth.

JULIAN

      Three cheers for Vulcano.

JACQUES

We hardly dare, alone, to beard the Baron, though.

VULCANO

Follow me, I will lead! (*To* MAUTPRÉ) 'Tis you
commence this strife!
Now pay your men their wage.

PIERRE, JULIAN, *and* JACQUES
      Our money!

VULCANO

      Or your life!
(*He, with the servants close behind him, rushes on the* BARON. CHICOT *and* NARCISSUS, *each with a sword, step in between*)

CHICOT

The first man who advances, dies.

VULCANO

      One of you go,
And take away those toys. 'Tis not for Vulcano
To fight with jesters.

ACT FOURTH

(*The servants are frightened at the determination of* CHICOT *and* NARCISSUS.)

JACQUES

But each seems to understand
Right well the way to use the weapon in his hand.

VULCANO

This is absurd, I swear! Varlets, but me no buts.
'T is time for deeds, not words. (*To* CHICOT) Your sword!

CHICOT, *with a menacing gesture*
Take care, it cuts.

VULCANO

Do you hear what I say? Disarm these two mad men!

JULIAN, *very gently*
An't please ye, sirs, your swords I'd have.

NARCISSUS, *laughing*
Why, take them then.

(*The three servants huddle together around* VULCANO)

CHICOT

Now, Vulcano, step forth. (*Looking him up and down*)
So 't is this braggart here,

This long, thin, scraggy loon whom all of you do fear.
This windbag whom I need but with my swordpoint prick
To empty him of words and gestures. This great stick
Of uselessness, this knave, this drunken jumping jack
Whom I—

VULCANO

I've heard enough. En garde! Come on, Crookback!
I'll cut your heart out and will have it cooked.

CHICOT
                           Oh, no!
You'll eat your own heart out with shame, my Vulcano,
When we have done with you. (*They cross swords*)

VULCANO
                Sa, ha! One!

CHICOT, *parrying his thrust*
                        Two! How now?
Your breath is coming somewhat laboured.

VULCANO
                        Tell me how
You would be killed!

ACT FOURTH

CHICOT

I think that I will live instead.

VULCANO

Die then.

CHICOT, *parrying*

See there. Had I but wished, your foolish head
Had I that moment cleft quite evenly in twain.

VULCANO, *contemptuously*

Actor!

CHICOT

'T is true I had not met with any brain.

VULCANO, *thrusting wildly*

Buffoon!

CHICOT

Take care, my friend. One more such thrust and we
Shall make a corpse of you.

NARCISSUS

Keep him alive for me.
I want a turn with him, he's given me offence.

CHICOT, *disarming* VULCANO

Then take him, Narcissus, and teach him how to
fence.

VULCANO, *looking at his sword on the ground*

Disarmed! By a Chicot!

NARCISSUS

Come, man, and let me try
If I can teach you how to fence and how to die.

JACQUES

Into my pouch I have slipped all pretence of pride,
Methinks 't is safer for us on the other side.

(JACQUES, PIERRE, *and* JULIAN *slip over unobtrusively to the group behind the* BARON)

NARCISSUS, *to* VULCANO

In carte shall I transfix you, or wouldst rather die
In tierce?

VULCANO

Look to yourself!

MAUTPRÉ, *in admiration*

He fences wondrously,
So does Chicot! I ne'er saw such men as these two.

BAROCO, *to himself*

I think I'll slip across and join the others, too.
(*He does so*)

NARCISSUS, *thrusting*

There!

VULCANO

There!

ACT FOURTH

NARCISSUS

Insulter of old men and maids, your tune
You now must change. Yield up your steel. (*He disarms him*)

BAROCO, *with a sigh of relief*
Phew! None too soon.

VULCANO

I'm done.

MAUTPRÉ, *to* NARCISSUS *and* CHICOT
I thank you, sirs.

CHICOT

Bind me that scurvy knave.
(PIERRE, JACQUES, *and* JULIAN *rush across and secure* VULCANO. BAROCO *follows them, carrying a piece of rope*)

VULCANO, *in reproachful astonishment to* BAROCO
You also?

BAROCO

Vulcano, I am not over brave
And so, as now it seems that one of us must die,
I thought it better that it should be you than I.
And so I change my coat.

THE JESTERS

VULCANO

>What foul ingratitude
From one whom I protected!

BAROCO

>Tush! Be not so rude,
I pray you. (*He flicks him with the rope end*)

MAUTPRÉ

Whence did you, young sirs, if I may ask,
Acquire your fencing?

OLIVER
They—

CHICOT

>Nay. It is time the mask
Were thrown aside. My lord, before you now, behold
Two men of your own rank, attracted by your gold.
De Chancenac's my name.

NARCISSUS

>Robert de Belfonte mine.

CHICOT, *taking off his hump*
As for this hump, I wore it as an outward sign
Of my infirmity of wit.—'T is false! I throw
It, false as his vaunted valour is, to Vulcano.

ACT FOURTH

MAUTPRÉ

But why, sirs, these disguises? And where is the gold
Of which you speak?

CHICOT

   De Mautpré, we were always told
That you were poor.

MAUTPRÉ, *bitterly*

  I see. And so that you should know,
And tell your friends that I in bitter sooth am so,
You came here.

CHICOT

  No, my lord. I pray you let me speak
Unto the end. We came a treasure here to seek.

MAUTPRÉ

A treasure here? Indeed!

CHICOT

   Aye! One more precious far
Than gold or jewelled trash.

MAUTPRÉ
who does not understand, but is very angry

   Enough, my lord. You are
Here under false pretence. And I have made a vow
That none should come within my castle walls. So
 now—

CHICOT

You bid us go. But let me name ere we depart
The treasure which we seek.

MAUTPRÉ
Well?

CHICOT
Your fair daughter's heart.
As de Belfonte and as de Chancenac we knew
That you would not admit us into speech with you,
So we assumed the jesters' garb and hither came
To woo and win Solange.

MAUTPRÉ
For shame, my lords, for shame!

SOLANGE, *to* OLIVER

He is of noble birth! His back as mine is straight!
Then 'tis no shame to love.

OLIVER, *to* SOLANGE
No longer need you wait
For your Prince Charming. He is here.

MAUTPRÉ
Nay, sirs, I know
Not how to speak my anger with you both!

ACT FOURTH 165

CHICOT, *to* OLIVER

Now go
And make the signal. (*Exit* OLIVER)

MAUTPRÉ

I have told you, sirs, that I
Live here in very real stress of poverty,
But we Mautprés are proud, and love our name too well
Our daughters into wedlock for your gold to sell.
You have been welcome here as jesters, but you came
As traitors, gentlemen, against de Mautpré's name.
Your swords have pardoned much. It was a youthful freak,
And of it I will in view of your youth not speak,
But now the jest is done. Your suit of no avail
Can ever be. Solange de Mautpré's not for sale.

CHICOT

But were you, good my lord, not poor, but rich?

MAUTPRÉ

Then I
Would welcome you. And now, farewell, sirs.

(*He rises and takes* SOLANGE's *hand.* CHICOT, *as she passes, whispers to her*)

CHICOT, *to* SOLANGE

        Prithee try
To meet me here anon.

SOLANGE

  I'll come.

(MAUTPRÉ *has been listening to the servants' pleas for pardon*)

JACQUES

      Lord, hear us swear
Renewed allegiance.

MAUTPRÉ

  Well, string up that braggart there
On high, and pardoned be. (*To* CHICOT *and* NARCISSUS) Each of you, sirs, our guest
Will till to-morrow be. I go to take my rest
Within my chamber. Come, Solange.

CHICOT, *whispers*

        I'll linger yet
Here for an hour. Forget not.

SOLANGE

    I will not forget.

(VULCANO, *after a struggle, is carried off into the castle dungeon through the postern door.* NARCISSUS *and* CHICOT *are left alone*)

ACT FOURTH

NARCISSUS

Well, I have loved and lost, it seems. And losing proved
That wit must triumph over beauty.

CHICOT, *meditatively*

Am I loved
Indeed by sweet Solange? Can one so wondrous sweet
As she return the love which at her tiny feet
My full heart pours?

NARCISSUS

Indeed she can. Why, friend, her throne
No queen of love would care to occupy alone.
She will come back. I'll leave you. (*Exit*)

OLIVER

Sir, the signal's made.

CHICOT

I thank you.

OLIVER

Here Solange comes. I will go. (*Exit*)

CHICOT

Afraid
Am I now that Solange my trick may disapprove.
What am I, after all, to win Solange's love?

(*Enter* SOLANGE. *She sits down without speaking. After a slight pause*)

CHICOT

Surely, sweet maid, because your poor Chicot must go,
You will not scorn him?

SOLANGE, *gently*
   You no longer are Chicot.

CHICOT

Oh, do not think, Solange, I prithee, that my ruse
Had for object an idle moment to amuse,
Or take me for a thief who came merely to pry
Into your heart, and steal your friendship only. I
Loved you, Solange, and sent Chicot here in my place
To win, if so he could, some little of your grace.
Then when upon your cheek mantled love's rosy shame,
Hoping, I sent Chicot away, and René came.
Believe me, dearest heart, and to me plight your troth.
Chicot has disappeared, René loves you for both.

SOLANGE, *tenderly*
In René dear, I love the wit of poor Chicot,

ACT FOURTH

Whose name I never shall forget. And always, so
Remembering, I shall deep down in my heart unite
My lovers twain into one long complete delight.
(*They kiss. Enter* OLIVER)

OLIVER
My lord René.
(SOLANGE, *without leaving* RENÉ's arms, *holds out a hand to* OLIVER)

SOLANGE
Old friend!

OLIVER
The fairy prince is here
At last I see. I pray all happiness, my dear,
The good God may upon your golden head downpour,
That you in joy may live with René evermore.

SOLANGE
My father we must tell.

CHICOT
That task, sweet, leave to me.

SOLANGE
That and my life, my lord, an you will have of me.

(DE CHANCENAC's *servant,* HUBERT, *appears on the pathway overlooking the keep*)

HUBERT

My lord! All's ready. The men with the chest are
  here.

CHICOT

Then let the play commence.

SOLANGE
                What play?

CHICOT
                    Nay, nay, my dear,
Your life you have but now entrusted all to me,
Wait then a little while, Solange, and you shall see.

HUBERT, *calling*

Holà! Below there! Is there nobody, I pray,
Who cares to carry good news to my lord Mautpré?

(*There is a great stir in the castle. Heads appear at
 the windows*)

JACQUES, *calling*

Good my lord!

NICOLE, *calling*
    My lord!

JULIAN
      Lord!

CHICOT, *to* HUBERT
          Right well have you begun;

ACT FOURTH

Bring presently the chest and then your task is done.

HUBERT

Baron de Mautpré!

MAUTPRÉ

Well, sir, why this loud outcry?

HUBERT

I bring good news.

MAUTPRÉ

Welcome! De Mautpré, sir, am I.
Who sends you?

HUBERT

I am come from Fol Bois, in Touraine,
Where my lord's walls run with the walls of your domain
And castle!

MAUTPRÉ

Castle! Why scarce do the old stones hold
Together now!

HUBERT

'T is sooth. Yet there has been found gold.

MAUTPRÉ

Gold? On my land?

HUBERT

My lord, deep buried in the ground

Beyond the castle walls, last week two peasants found
A chest with treasure, and my lord did forthwith say,
This is the buried treasure of old de Mautpré.

MAUTPRÉ

Old?

HUBERT

Old Lord Hector.

MAUTPRÉ, *to* OLIVER

There, I knew it must be true!
(*To* HUBERT)
Where is this treasure chest? Have you brought it with you?

HUBERT

Yes, my lord.

MAUTPRÉ

Bring it down. You, varlets (*to* PIERRE, JACQUES, *and* JULIAN), were afraid
That your wages would ne'er by de Mautpré be paid.

JACQUES

My lord!

MAUTPRÉ

And you rebelled. It was enough, I trow,

ACT FOURTH

That Mautpré pledged his word. The gold you shall
see now
And finger some of it, although your unbelief
Refused me in my hour of need the least relief.

JULIAN
Pardon us, good my lord.

RENÉ, *to* OLIVER
      His fable become truth,
De Mautpré, as I thought he would, believes forsooth.

(HUBERT *appears again on the pathway above the keep wall. He is followed by four men and a horse with the treasure chest on its back*)

JACQUES
Here is the treasure.

MAUTPRÉ
    Bring it, my friends, down the wall.

HUBERT
'T is heavy.

PIERRE
  Here's the stairway.

MAUTPRÉ
      Do not let it fall.

NARCISSUS, *to* CHICOT
Cleverly done, René.

SOLANGE, *to* CHICOT

    Can I be worth, my lord,
So great a chest of gold?

CHICOT

    Now will your father's board
Welcome me once again, for he is rich and he
My treasure thrice returns giving Solange to me.
(*To* MAUTPRÉ)
Well, good my lord, I see fortune has smiled on you.

NARCISSUS

Will you not also smile, sir, now upon us two?
We stand again before you, humble suitors, and —

CHICOT

Each asks that priceless gift, the sweet Solange's hand.

MAUTPRÉ

Speak boldly up and choose, Solange, be not afraid,
One of these two young lords.

SOLANGE

    Father, my choice is made.
(*She gives her hand to* CHICOT)
But I would crave a boon.

MAUTPRÉ

    Ask. Ere you ask, 't is thine.

ACT FOURTH

SOLANGE

Then let Vulcano live! Hast thou thought, father mine,
That if the gallows-tree should with his body's weight
Break,—it's worm-eaten,—he crook-backed instead of straight
Like my René here might become?

MAUTPRÉ

Well, Vulcano
May leave the castle with his good friend Baroco.

SOLANGE

I thank you, sir.

RENÉ

And I.

OLIVER, *to* JACQUES

Now let loud trumpet blast
Summon the countryside here to a great repast
Where all shall be made welcome. Let our vassals know
Fair Solange is betrothed to René—

SOLANGE, *laughing*

And Chicot.

CURTAIN

Featured Titles from Westphalia Press

Peasant Art in Sweden, Lapland and Iceland
by Charles Holme

This particular work offers a carefully chosen selection of both the decorative and fine arts of Sweden, Iceland, and the northern most region of Finland. A comprehensive survey, it includes paintings, jewelry, textiles, metalwork, carving, furniture and pottery.

The Rise of the Book Plate: An Exemplative of the Art
by W. G. Bowdoin, Introduction by Henry Blackwel

Bookplates were made to denote ownership and hopefully steer the volume back to the rightful shelf if borrowed. They often contained highly stylized writing, drawings, coat of arms, badges or other images of interest to the owner.

The Art of Table Setting, Ancient and Modern
by Claudia Quigley Murphy

The arrangement of a table in terms of cutlery, arrangement, serving style, and timing of courses has changed a great deal over time and now is enjoying renewed interest. The History of the Art of Tablesetting was written by a true expert in the field, Claudia Quigley Murphy.

Understanding Art: Hendrik Willem Van Loon's
How To Look At Pictures by Hendrik Willem Van
Loon, Introduction by Daniel Gutierrez-Sandoval

Hendrik Willem van Loon was a Dutch-American professor, journalist, prolific writer, and illustrator. His most famous work, "The Story of Mankind" earned him the prestigious John Newbery Medal.

The Etchings of Rembrandt: A Study and History
by P. G. Hamerton

Philip Gilbert Hamerton (1834-1894) was an Englishman who was devoted to the arts in numerous forms. Due to the praise, Hamerton stuck with art criticism, and went on to write other works. He also wrote novels, biographies, and reflections on society.

Lankes, His Woodcut Bookplates by Wilbur Macey Stone

Julius John Lankes was born in Buffalo, New York in 1884, and became a prolific woodcut print artist, as well as an author and professor. As a child, he enjoyed working with the scraps of wood his father brought home from the lumber mill where he was employed. Lankes had a lifelong interest in art.

Los Dibujos de Heriberto Juarez / The Drawings of Heriberto Juarez, Edited by Paul Rich

That the drawings here are from life in México is not surprising because Juárez is constantly, and at times impishly, putting art into life and getting art from life. He doesn't think of art as some thing that is done just in a studio or for that matter kept in museums and looked at on Sundays.

The History of Photography: Carl W. Ackerman's George Eastman by Carl W. Ackerman, Introduction by Daniel Gutierrez-Sandoval

The life of George Eastman is very much a part of the history of contemporary photography. Founder of the Eastman Kodak Company, Eastman was an enthusiastic photographer himself who became instrumental in bringing photography to the mainstream.

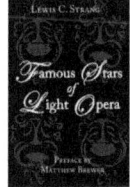

Famous Stars of Light Opera by Lewis C. Strang, Introduction by Matthew Brewer

Strang's attempts to quantify the humorous elements of each performer, as well as quotes from the performers themselves attempting to explain their own success, are an interesting exercise in attempting to explain the inexplicable.

Wood Sculpture: From Ancient Egypt to the End of the Gothic Period by Alfred Maskell F.S.A.

Alfred Maskell was an artist, primarily a photographer, who worked tirelessly to advance the art. Maskell, along with Robert Memachy, helped to develop the gum-bichromate printing, which is able to create a unique painterly image from negatives. This work highlights a variety of wood-based art over time.

westphaliapress.org

www.ingramcontent.com/pod-product-compliance
Lightning Source LLC
Chambersburg PA
CBHW061323040426
42444CB00011B/2750